MEDIAEVAL
& RENAISSANCE
MANUSCRIPTS

MEDIAEVAL & RENAISSANCE MANUSCRIPTS

Major Acquisitions of
The Pierpont Morgan Library
1924-1974

NEW YORK

COPYRIGHT © 1974 BY THE PIERPONT MORGAN LIBRARY

29 EAST 36 STREET, NEW YORK, N.Y. 10016

PHOTOGRAPHS BY CHARLES PASSELA AND FRANK DROUIN

PRINTED IN THE UNITED STATES OF AMERICA

LIBRARY OF CONGRESS CATALOGUE CARD NUMBER 73-92929

ISBN 87598-045-7

*

CONTENTS

VII

PREFACE

ABOUT ten years after The Pierpont Morgan Library was incorporated in the State of New York as a public library, Seymour de Ricci published a census of mediaeval and Renaissance manuscripts in the United States and Canada in which he wrote that the collection in the Morgan Library was "the most extensive and the most beautifully selected series of manuscripts existing on the American Continent, and it may truthfully claim to be superior in general quality to all but three or four of the greatest national libraries of the Old World." This statement has often been quoted, but it deserves repetition here, for it expresses the standard of excellence against which the Library has continued to measure its acquisitions of additional manuscripts. These manuscripts acquired since 1924 are worthy of joining that distinguished and "most beautifully selected series" which existed in the Library before its incorporation. The present book illustrates the outstanding achievement of J. P. Morgan and the Trustees, of Belle da Costa Greene and Frederick B. Adams, Jr., the Curators, and Fellows who have maintained the pre-eminence in America of the Morgan manuscript collections. They have insured that the Library is also a leading research center for the study of mediaeval and Renaissance manuscripts, and that it has given pleasure to a large public through exhibitions and publications. In these the Library has made important innovations which have enabled hundreds of thousands of people to enjoy all of the pages of painting in the finest mediaeval books.

The acquisitions which are described and illustrated in this book are therefore only part of the record of this department. It has fulfilled the terms of the State charter: ". . . to preserve, protect and give permanence to the collections . . . to render them available, under suitable regulations and restrictions having regard to their nature and value, to scholars and persons engaged in the work of research and to those interested in literature, art and kindred subjects, to disseminate and contribute to the advancement of useful information and knowledge . . . ”(Chapter 83 of the Laws of 1924, the State of New York, 26 March 1924). The collection of mediaeval manuscripts was the special interest of both Pierpont and J. P. Morgan, and of Miss Greene. The Library has also been most fortunate in its curators who have brought distinction to the study and publication of mediaeval manuscripts in this place: Miss Meta P. Harrsen, who came to the Library in 1922; John Plummer, her successor, who came here in 1954 and is now Curator of Mediaeval and Renaissance Manuscripts and Research Fellow; and William M. Voelkle, his Associate Curator. The introduction and essays which follow are Mr. Voelkle's, but he has drawn on the scholarship of his predecessors and especially his colleague, John Plummer, from whose critical reading and valuable suggestions the catalogue has greatly benefited.

Charles Ryskamp, Director

INTRODUCTION

WHEN, in the last year of the last century Pierpont Morgan (1837–1913) acquired his first illuminated manuscripts, he laid the foundation for a collection which in our century would contribute substantially toward the development of the cultural and intellectual life of this country, and especially toward the appreciation and study of illuminated manuscripts. "Prior to the formation of this collection by the late Mr. Pierpont Morgan," wrote Walter S. Cook, "there were no scholars in this country who had specialized in the field of illuminated manuscripts or recognized their place and importance in the history of painting; nor was the subject included in the curriculum of any American university, whereas today individual students are making research in these special fields and extensive courses are given at Harvard, Princeton, Columbia, New York, and other universities." Charles Rufus Morey enlarged on these sentiments when he wrote that various scholarly "studies and publications would not have been possible without the establishment of this collection in America. The significance of the foregoing is greater than at first appears, because . . . the various researches that cluster around the Morgan collection have been, in a sense, the first which have made American scholarship in mediaeval archaeology recognized in Europe as an important factor in the future development of the subject. . . . There is scarcely a phase of the art . . . which can be fully illustrated and understood at present without reference to the Morgan manuscripts. . . . The importance of this collection lies not only in its extent, but in the first-rate quality of the specimens."

The growing awareness of the importance of illuminated manuscripts, both as artistic achievements and cultural documents, has unfortunately also been accompanied by a number of side effects which served to make their acquisition more difficult over the years. Now regarded on a par with painting and sculpture, they command comparable prices on the market.

Their increasing scarcity is also an important factor. The foregoing reasons, coupled with the "manuscript drain" that certain European countries have been experiencing, has led to the practice of designating manuscripts as "national treasures," making their exportation impossible. Nevertheless, since the Library began its public life half a century ago, it has managed to acquire, by purchase or gift, 283 manuscripts, which in general quality and importance are on a par with the 673 volumes which the Library already had when it was founded in 1924 by J. P. Morgan in memory of his father. It should also be added, that, in spite of the increasing rarity of important manuscripts on the market, the quality of these acquisitions has remained remarkably consistent over the years.

Exactly fifty years ago William M. Ivins of the Metropolitan Museum organized an exhibition entitled "The Arts of the Book," to which the newly founded Library generously lent 104 of its finest illuminated manuscripts. The Library did so because it felt a strong obligation to display its treasures to the public, an obligation which it could not itself meet for another four years, when its own exhibition hall was constructed as a gift of its founder. While this was not the first exhibition of the Library's treasures —a smaller one had been held slightly earlier at the New York Public Library—it was the first time that some idea of the breadth and excellence of the collection was presented to the public. "That only one institution," said William Ivins, "should have been able, and with ease, to contribute from its own collection such an unrivalled and complete historic series of books and manuscripts made over the period of eight centuries, during which bookmaking in many respects reached its artistic culmination, was perhaps the most astonishing thing brought forth by the exhibition. For the first time the people of New York were able to appreciate with their own eyes the fact that their city contained one of the great collections of beautiful books in the world." What Ivins said of the collection in 1924 could be said of the acquisitions since then. The great accomplishment of the Library during the course of its public life, through the efforts of its three directors, Belle da Costa Greene (1924–1948), Frederick B. Adams, Jr. (1948–1969), and now Charles Ryskamp, is that now a new "Arts of the Book" exhibition of comparable beauty and historic importance could be assembled in which each manuscript would have been acquired since that time.

In such an exhibition, manuscripts spanning ten centuries could be seen, and from them much could be learned about how earlier man lived, what he read and thought, and how he used and contributed to knowledge. One would see, in admirable examples, the different ways in which he wrote, decorated, and bound his books over those centuries. Among the early centers of illumination represented would be those of Reims, Tours, Lorsch, Corvey, and St. Bertin. Manuscripts from such centers as Canterbury, St. Albans, Bury St. Edmunds, Salzburg, Weingarten, and Seitenstetten would also be included. The Gothic and Renaissance centers would be too numerous to mention. Artists' names before the fourteenth century are rare, but a leaf by W. de Brailes of about 1240 would be represented. From the fourteenth and fifteenth centuries would be manuscripts illuminated by Niccolò da Bologna, the Master of the St. George Codex, Michelino da Besozzo, Jean Fouquet, Jean Colombe, Jean Bourdichon, the Master of Catherine of Cleves, the Master of Edward IV, Nikolaus of Brünn, and Jacob Elsner. The books themselves would be diversified: aside from Bibles, there would be all kinds of service books, such as Sacramentaries, Missals, Lectionaries, Graduals, Ordinals, Breviaries, Antiphonaries, Psalters, Psalters–Books of Hours, Books of Hours; various theological works and commentaries; lives of the saints and other forms of devotional literature. Important works of the classical authors would also be represented, including Carolingian copies as well as humanist manuscripts. There would be scientific manuscripts dealing with astrology, astronomy, medicine, plants, animals, and minerals; and works of a more practical nature telling when and how to plant, how to take care of horses, how to hunt and fight. There would be works of historical interest, such as biographies and chronicles. Works relating to

XIII

law, exploration, and cartography would also be present. And lastly, for pleasure, would be the mediaeval romances, although these were frequently moralizing as well.

Much as we would like to show all of the manuscripts acquired in the last fifty years, we cannot do so, and must content ourselves with less than one-fifth of that number. Thus we have selected, primarily for their visual appeal, forty-nine codices and a single leaf to stand for the whole. These fifty items—each a witness to the achievement of the Library as a public institution—are illustrated in this publication, which is issued in honor of its fiftieth anniversary. Since they are roughly chronologically arranged and briefly described, no further discussion of them is required here. While the other manuscripts are all described in works cited in the appended bibliographical note, a number of the textual manuscripts and single leaves not considered for selection are of sufficient importance that they deserve special mention. Among the textual manuscripts are two of the Carolingian period, both dating from the ninth century. The first is Pliny the Elder's Natural History (Books I-XVII; M.871) which was written at Lorsch, and is one of the earliest copies of that text to have survived. The second, and more important, is the oldest and most complete copy known of the Fables of Phaedrus (M.906), which was written in France. Pierre Pithou owned the manuscript in 1596, when he published the first critical edition of the text. A third manuscript, also of a classical author, contains the *Topica* of Aristotle (M.758), and is probably the oldest surviving representative of the manuscript family from which Boethius made his Latin translation. The manuscript, in Greek, dates from about the tenth or eleventh century. A still later document for the transmission and preservation of classical texts is a fourteenth-century manuscript containing a selection of Ovid's works (M.810), which was written in Italy and belonged to Coluccio Salutati (1331–1406), the famous humanist and friend of Petrarch. Of great historical interest is the Chronicle of William Marshal (1147–1219; M.888), a thirteenth-century English manuscript which provides most of what we know about the man who was the regent of England following the death of King John in 1216. A final textual manuscript (M.819), written in Italy at the end of the thirteenth century, contains one of the most important collections of Provençal poetry that exists. The manuscript is also one of the finest illustrated manuscripts of troubadour poetry.

Except for a very recent acquisition (our number 49), single leaves have not been considered in this publication, but a few of the more important examples should be mentioned here. The earliest is a Gospel leaf (M.874) from the Codex Petropolitanus (today mostly preserved in the Public Library of Leningrad, Codex N), a sixth-century manuscript on purple vellum, made in Syria, and written in gold and silver. A leaf (M.724) with a cycle of Biblical scenes in nineteen compartments, possibly made at Canterbury or St. Albans in the twelfth century, is one of four such leaves which survive. One other is also in the Morgan Library (M.521). Another English leaf (M.913), but from about the middle of the next century, was illuminated by W. de Brailes, contains scenes from the infancy of Christ, and comes from a dismembered Psalter which must have been his masterpiece. The largest of the single leaves (65 x 20½ inches) is a map of Palestine (M.877) attributed to Pietro Vesconte, which was made in Venice about 1300. Only recently discovered, this monument of cartography—the oldest nonschematic map in America—remained the model, directly and indirectly, for maps of the Holy Land for many centuries. A splendid God in Majesty (M.742) from a dismembered *Laudario*, or collection of hymns, was illuminated in the workshop of Pacino di Bonaguida. Four magnificent leaves illustrating the Decretals of Pope Gregory IX (M.716.1–4) were illuminated in Bologna in the second half of the fourteenth century. Lastly, mention should be made of three leaves from a Missal that was illuminated, before 1381, in the workshop of Master Bertram of Minden, the most famous painter in Germany in his time.

A number of the manuscripts also contain bindings of exceptional interest for the history of that art. In addition to the four glorious jewelled bindings discussed in this catalogue (our numbers 8, 9, 20, and 21), there are also bindings by Johannes Hagmayr of Ulm (M.793), Clovis Ève (M.927), a superb Bohemian *cuir cisilé* binding of the fourteenth century (M.822), and apparently the earliest monastic binding (about 1410) stamped with the name of the monastery where it was bound, Saint Justina of Padua (M.859).

Finally, a word ought to be said about the catalogue and the entries themselves. Manuscripts, unlike paintings or drawings, cannot be easily described. It is impossible to grasp their totality in a few words or by a single reproduction. While a miniature can be appreciated as a single painting, each takes on a far greater meaning when viewed in terms of the whole. The cycles and decorative schemes have their own systems of hierarchies, themes, and variations, and to understand the whole one must turn the pages, just as one must listen to the entire symphony to understand the relationship of the whole to the parts or to savor the unfolding of its movements. Here, however, we must content ourselves with brief descriptions and representative illustrations. Although these descriptions are not intended to be scholarly—aiming rather at a more general public—they represent and incorporate the contributions of hundreds of scholars who have communicated their discoveries about these manuscripts in print or orally. To acknowledge them all would be to write a history of the discipline. Problems regarding the attribution, dating, and localization of manuscripts are difficult, and opinions are often tentative. If the material given here stimulates the eye and mind, and perhaps even prompts further research, moving ahead our knowledge and appreciation for illuminated manuscripts, then the primary function of this catalogue will have been served.

William Voelkle

CATALOGUE

1

PSALM 68

England, second half of the VIII century [M.776, fol. 27]

According to tradition St. Jerome made three translations of the Psalter: the *Romanum*, *Gallicanum* or Vulgate, and the *Hebraicum*. This text is the first, a correction of the old Latin translation made from the Greek Septuagint, which is still used in St. Peter's, Rome. The second, a further correction using the Hebrew Psalter, was the version most commonly used in the liturgy down to the present day. The third, a fresh translation from the Hebrew, was apparently never used liturgically. It was the *Romanum* Psalter, of which only a few other eighth-century copies exist, that St. Augustine brought with him to England at the end of the sixth century. Here the first line of Psalm 68 has been written in large display letters to mark one of the divisions of the Psalter: *Salvum me fac* (Save me). These letters, ornamented in the so-called Hiberno-Saxon style which flourished in Ireland and Britain in the seventh and eight centuries, are composed of the familiar interlace, spiral, and animal forms found in such well-known manuscripts as the Lindisfarne Gospels (London, British Museum, Cotton Ms. Nero D.IV) and the Book of Durrow (Dublin, Trinity College Library, Ms.57). Some of the pages also contain Anglo-Saxon glosses, which are of interest because they provide linguistic evidence for the development of the English language.

PSALTER, *in Latin, with some Anglo-Saxon and Latin glosses. England, probably Mercia or Canterbury; second half of the* VIII *century. 94 leaves (12 x 9 in.; 306 x 230 mm.). 4 lines written in large ornamented letters and 124 other initials. Purchased in 1932.*

ecce dabit uocem suam uocem uirtutis suae

date honorem dō ⁖ ·   ſibur

Super iſrahel magnificentia eiuſ & uirtuſ eiuſ innu·

mirabiliſ dſ inſciſ ſuiſ dſ iſrahel ipſe dabit

uirtutem & fortitudinem plebiſ ſuae benedictuſ dſ·

Aluumme fac

dſ quo introierunt aquae

uſque adanimam meam infixuſ ſū

inlimum profundi & non eſt ſubſtantia ⁖ ·

Ueni inaltitudinem mariſ & tempeſtaſ demerſit me ·

Laboraui clamanſ raucae factae ſunt·

fauceſ meae defecerunt oculi mei

dum ſpero indm meum ⁖ ·

multiplicatiſunt ſupra capilloſ capitiſ

mei · qui oderunt me gratiſ ⁖ ·

Confortatiſunt ſupra me qui me perſequuntur

inimici mei iniuſte· quae non rapui tunc exſolueba᷑

O ſcſ ſciſ inſipientiam meam & delicta

mea· a te non ſunt abſcondita ·

Non erubeſccant inme qui te exſpectant·

                    ne ſer gaſ

dne dſuirtutam non reuereantur

2

ST. JOHN THE EVANGELIST

France, about 860 [M.862, fol. 144v]

Although this book is not as profusely illustrated as some Carolingian Gospels, it is, nevertheless, important as an early specimen of the so-called Franco-Saxon school. The chief center of this school is thought to have been the Benedictine monastery of St. Amand, the likely source of this codex. The manuscript may have had the same proto-type as the Gospels of Francis II (Paris, Bibliothèque Nationale, lat.257), which has the same inscriptions surrounding the evangelist symbols. These inscriptions are taken from the writings of the Spanish bishop Theodulph, who, with Alcuin, was one of the most important scholars called to Charlemagne's court. In this manuscript each Gospel con-tains four pages of decoration except for that of Matthew, where a leaf has been excised. The first of these, always a verso, has an evangelist portrait. The second, a facing page, has a title page which announces the text that is to follow. The third and fourth, also facing pages with corresponding borders, contain the opening words of the Gospel it-self. Of the four evangelist portraits only one depicts the evangelist writing his Gospel in gold letters, that of John, whose Gospel begins with the glorification of the word of God: "In the beginning was the Word, and the Word was with God, and the Word was God."

GOSPELS, *in Latin. Northern France, probably St. Amand; about 860. 193 leaves (9½ x 7½ in.; 240 x 190 mm.). 12 decorated canon tables, 4 full-page miniatures, 4 decorated incipit pages, 6 framed text pages. Purchased on the Belle da Costa Greene Fund, 1952.*

3

ST. JOHN THE EVANGELIST

France, between 845 and 882 [M.728, fol. 141v]

The most distinctive and perhaps the most influential of all the Carolingian schools of painting was that of Reims (see also our numbers 6, 7, and 12) which produced the Utrecht Psalter (Utrecht, Bibliotheek der Rijksuniversiteit, Ms.Script.eccl.484), one of the most famous of all mediaeval manuscripts. This Gospels, written in gold Carolingian minuscules, also ranks as one of the most important productions of that school and is one of the finest of all Carolingian manuscripts. It was probably made at the abbey of St. Remi, where it remained until the end of the eighteenth century. A comparison of its St. John with that of the Franco-Saxon manuscript reproduced on the preceding page is revealing. The Reims John is less removed from ancient models, preserving a feeling of strength and modelling; it adds, however, that nervous line—the hallmark of the Reims school—which imparts to the figure a sense of excitement and ecstasy. While the Gospel of Loisel in Paris (Bibliothèque Nationale, lat.17968) has very similarly decorated canon tables and its evangelists are of the same type, they do not share the richness of detail of those found in this manuscript.

GOSPELS, *in Latin. Reims, France; during the time of Archbishop Hincmar (845–882). 192 leaves (12 ⅛ x 10 ⅛ in.; 303 x 258 mm.). 4 full-page miniatures, 4 decorated incipit pages, and 12 canon pages decorated with birds, men, and satyrs. Purchased in 1927.*

INITIAL PAGE OF THE GOSPEL OF ST. LUKE

France, between 857 and 862 [M.860, fol. 96]

Carolingian Gospels do not always have evangelist portraits preceding each Gospel. In this manuscript, for example, two exceptionally refined ornamented pages introduce each of the four Gospels: the first is a kind of title page and the second, the initial page, contains the beginning of the Gospel itself. Here the letter Q, of *Quoniam quidem multi conati sunt ordinare*, begins the Gospel of Luke. The designs and ornamental forms in the manuscript, one of the most splendid produced in the scriptorium of St. Martin at Tours, are derived from a slightly earlier Gospels made there for the Emperor Lothaire (Paris, Bibliothèque Nationale, lat.266). The monastery of St. Martin, the center of the Tours school of painting, had come into prominence when Alcuin of York, in the years 796–804, transformed it into an important center for the study, revision, and copying of the Bible. While Tours was perhaps the most prolific of all the Carolingian schools of painting, that of Reims (see our number 3) was the most influential, especially in England (see our numbers 6, 7, and 12).

GOSPELS, *in Latin. Monastery of St. Martin at Tours, France; between 857 and 862. 206 leaves (11 ½ x 9 in.; 293 x 229 mm.). 6 decorated canon tables, 5 decorated title pages, 4 large illuminated initials. Purchased with the assistance of the Fellows, 1952.*

VO
NAM
QVDE

MVLTI
CONATISVNT
ORDINARE

5

INITIAL PAGE OF THE GOSPEL OF ST. JOHN

Germany, middle of the X century [M.755, fol. 157v]

Since the German monastery of Corvey was a foundation of the French monastery of Corbie, near Amiens, it is not surprising that the text, scripts, and ornamentation of manuscripts produced there should show some affinity with the productions of the mother house. The textual variants of this Gospels, for example, have been found in the Gospel text used at the monastery of Corbie. Although one of the best examples of the luxurious manuscripts from Corvey, this codex, like the Tours Gospels (our number 4), has no miniatures. Nevertheless, its seventeen illuminated text pages provide ample compensation: some contain lavishly burnished gold ornamentation, others exhibit richly decorated backgrounds with patterns of foliage, birds, and animals that resemble Byzantine textiles. Although some of these pages are easily legible, others are not, such as the beginning of the Gospel of John reproduced here. While the letters of the first two words *In principio* are obscured by interlace, the second two words *erat verbum* can be clearly read at the top of the page. Stylistic parallels can be found in four other manuscripts, all of which are in the same group: Reims, Bibliothèque Municipale, Ms.10; Baltimore, Walters Art Gallery, w.751 (the four leaves were formerly in the A. Chester Beatty collection); Wolfenbüttel, Herzog-August-Bibliothek, Cod.Guelf.84.3 Aug. fol.; and New York, New York Public Library, Astor Ms.1.

GOSPELS, *in Latin. Abbey of Corvey, Westphalia, Germany; middle of the* X *century. 201 leaves (13¾ x 10¼ in.; 350 x 261 mm.). 16 decorated canon tables, 17 illuminated introductory text pages, 1 decorated initial. Purchased in 1929.*

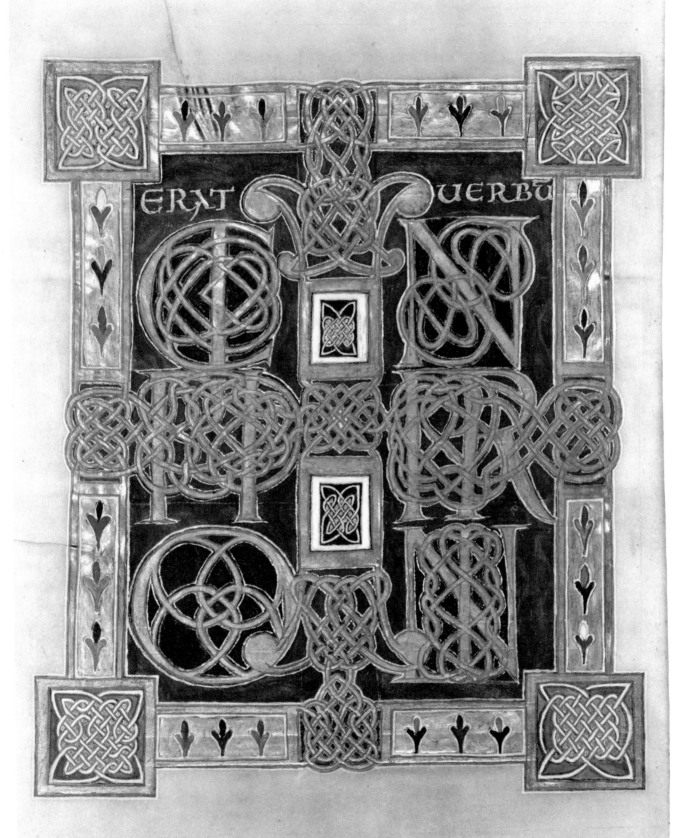

ST. MATTHEW THE EVANGELIST

England, end of the X century [M.869, fol. 17v]

This portrait of Matthew is representative of the four drawings of evangelists in this manuscript: each evangelist is enclosed, with his symbol, in a complicated architectural framework, is shown in the act of writing his Gospel, and is accompanied by an appropriate quotation from the fifth-century Christian poet Sedulius. These drawings and especially those that adorn the canon tables are not only the inheritors of the antique-inspired Reims style as found in the Utrecht Psalter (Utrecht, Bibliotheek der Rijksuniversiteit, Ms.Script.eccl.484), but rank among the finest and most important English drawings of their time. The closest stylistic parallels of the drawings, some of which are compositionally and iconographically unique, are found in a Prudentius *Psychomachia* in Cambridge (Corpus Christi College, Ms.23) which may have been made in Malmesbury.

GOSPELS, *in Latin. England, probably in the West; end of the* X *century. 167 leaves (11⅞ x 7½ in.; 302 x 191 mm.). 5 full-page miniatures, 8 quarter-page drawings over the canon tables, 4 decorated incipit pages. Purchased with the assistance of the Fellows and the special assistance of Mr. William S. Glazier, 1954.*

ST. LUKE THE EVANGELIST

France, second half of the X century [*M.827, fol. 66v*]

This Gospels, known as the Anhalt Gospels because the codex was already in the library of the Dukes of Anhalt by the twelfth century, is decorated in at least two different styles: most of the decorated text pages and canon tables are by artists of the center in northern France which produced the text, but the evangelist portraits, English in style, are evidently the work of an itinerant Englishman or a French artist trained in England. The same artist also painted the miniatures in a Gospels from the Abbey of St. Bertin which is now in the Bibliothèque Municipale in Boulogne (Ms.11.) The St. Luke reproduced here (like the St. Matthew on the preceding page) provides yet another example of the influence of the Reims school of painting upon tenth-century English illumination. The portrait of Luke is also interesting because of its peculiar iconography: Luke is seated frontally, with his feet resting on a disc; in his veiled right hand he holds a book, and in his left a palm. While the four corners may originally have contained the symbols of the evangelists, only one is now clearly visible, that of the ox, the appropriate symbol for Luke. By way of explanation it has been suggested that the model for this miniature may have been a Christ in Majesty. Other miniatures related in style can be found in a number of English manuscripts, such as the late tenth-century Psalter in London (British Museum, Harley Ms.2904).

GOSPELS, *in Latin. Northern France, probably at the Abbey of St. Bertin; second half of the* x *century. 128 leaves (14 ¼ x 10 ¼ in.; 362 x 261 mm.). 4 full-page miniatures, 14 decorated canon tables, 4 decorated incipit pages, and 6 other decorated text pages. Purchased on the Lewis Cass Ledyard Fund, 1948.*

8

ST. JOHN THE EVANGELIST

England, about 1020 [*M.709, fol. 122v*]

Although this splendid Gospels was once thought to have been made for Countess
Judith of Flanders (1032–1094), this possibility is now precluded by an earlier dating of
the manuscript, which, along with a group of stylistically related manuscripts, may have
been made in Canterbury about 1020. There is no doubt, however, that it was later in
her possession, for in 1094 she bequeathed it and other manuscripts including our number 9 to Weingarten Abbey, the ancestral monastery of her second husband, Welf IV,
Duke of Bavaria, and her burial place. In its new home the manuscript was to have an
influence on certain manuscripts produced at the abbey during the twelfth century,
especially a Missal now in Fulda (Landesbibliothek, Ms.Aa.6), which has adopted the
rich acanthus borders that surround its evangelist portraits. Shown here is the portrait of
John, who, holding his pen and knife, is engaged in the act of writing his Gospel in gold
letters. Unlike our number 2, however, all of the words which he has written can be
clearly read: *In principio erat verbum.* The manuscript's jewelled cover, which contains a
large gold repoussé plaque depicting Christ in a mandorla, and four smaller ones (in
surrounding spandrels) with the evangelists' symbols, is neither contemporary nor English. It was probably made in northern France or Belgium about a half of a century later,
and is frequently compared with the repoussé Christ from the shrine of St. Hadelin in
the church of St. Martin in Visé.

GOSPELS, *in Latin. England, probably Canterbury; about 1020. 154 leaves (11 ½ x 7 ½ in.; 293 x 191 mm.).
5 full-page miniatures, 4 decorated incipit pages with corresponding full borders. Purchased in 1926.*

9

ST. MARK THE EVANGELIST

England, middle of the XI century [M.708, fol. 26v]

Although this Gospels and a number of related manuscripts have been attributed to the Winchester school, all evidence indicates that the manuscripts were made at some other and still unidentified center. Typical of mid-eleventh-century English illumination, their figural style represents a further stage toward the development of the Romanesque in England than that exhibited by our preceding entry. This development can be clearly seen by comparing the portrait of Mark shown here with that of a John (preceding page) made some thirty years earlier. The more elegant and refined John, rendered in delicate shades of pink, yellow, and blue, gives way to a broader and more vigorous Mark, who is painted in somewhat darker and more somber colors. Both evangelists, however, are painted on uncolored vellum, giving a white background to the figures. The closest stylistic parallels are found in three portraits in a Gospels, apparently executed by the same workshop, which is now in Monte Cassino (Archivio della Badia, Ms.437). The manuscript's jewelled cover, made about the same time or slightly later, is divided into two registers depicting Christ in Majesty and the Crucifixion. The figures, which are silver gilt and separately cast, are important for the history of both English goldsmiths' work and sculpture of the time. The Morgan manuscript, like our number 8, was owned by Countess Judith of Flanders, who bequeathed it to Weingarten Abbey, the ancestral monastery of her second husband, Welf IV, Duke of Bavaria, whom she married in 1071.

GOSPELS, *in Latin. England; middle of the* XI *century. 86 leaves (11 ⅝ x 7 ¾ in.; 296 x 197 mm.). 4 full-page miniatures and 4 illuminated incipit pages. Purchased in 1926.*

10

DEPOSITION

Austria, first half of the XI century [M.781, fol. 223v]

The Salzburg school of illumination, unlike many of the other Ottonian schools, evolved almost without a break into the Romanesque style of the twelfth century. Three important and splendid manuscripts in the Morgan Library illustrate aspects of the eleventh-century stages of that development. The present Gospels, dating from the first half of the century, is the earliest of these, and still retains characteristics of the art practiced under the Ottos, an art that had been influenced by Byzantium as a result of such events as the marriage of the Emperor Otto II, in 972, to Theophanou, a Byzantine princess. The other two are decidedly more Romanesque, for the figures exhibit a new sense of substance, modelling, and energy. Whereas both of these are closely related in date, and separated from the present Gospels by at least a quarter of a century, the Lectionary in the William S. Glazier collection (on deposit in the Library as G.44) is clearly earlier than that of Custos Perhtolt (M.780), the next entry in this book. While some of this manuscript's evangelist portraits and canon table decoration have been related to the Michael-beueren Gospels in Munich (Staatsbibliothek, Clm.8272), there is also a stylistic connection with a somewhat later Lectionary in the same city (Clm.15713). The unusual Deposition shown here—by the finer of the two hands that can be distinguished—and the other miniatures do not form a cycle at the beginning of the text, but are scattered throughout. This Gospels and the Lectionary of Custos Perhtolt remained at the abbey of St. Peter's (as Codex a.x.6 and a.vi.55), where they were made, until their acquisition by the Library.

GOSPELS, *in Latin. Benedictine monastery of St. Peter, Salzburg, Austria; first half of the XI century. 227 leaves (13½ x 10½ in.; 343 x 266 mm.). 7 full-page and 16 smaller miniatures, 18 canon tables, 4 decorated incipit pages. Purchased on the Lewis Cass Ledyard Fund, 1933.*

11

NATIVITY AND ANNUNCIATION TO THE SHEPHERDS

Austria, second half of the XI century [M.780, fol. 4]

According to its colophon this manuscript was made and dedicated by a certain Custos Perhtolt "to the bearer of the keys of heaven . . . as an expiation for all sins committed by him." While this curator Perhtolt has not been identified, though other manuscripts have been attributed to him (the closest is a Gospel in the monastery of Admont, Ms.511), there is little doubt that the "bearer of keys" refers to St. Peter, the patron of the abbey in Salzburg where the manuscript was produced. The Lectionary, which represents a more advanced stage than the preceding Gospels in the transition from the Ottonian to the Romanesque periods, is stylistically closer to the Glazier Lectionary (G.44), especially in the facial types. Like the Gospels, it is also related to the Lectionary in Munich (Staats-bibliothek, Clm.15713), but not so much for stylistic reasons. The similarities have more to do with the form, selection, and arrangement of its cycle of miniatures. The Nativity which is shown here also includes the Annunciation to the Shepherds and the Midwife Washing the Christ Child. The necessity for the washing of the child was much disputed by theologians, who argued that Christ's birth was as pure as his conception. More than being washed, they contended that his pure and spotless body washed the waters, constituting a reference to baptism. Such discussions may well have prompted the baptismal character of this representation.

LECTIONARY OF THE GOSPELS, *in Latin. Benedictine monastery of St. Peter, Salzburg, Austria; second half of the* XI *century; made by Custos Perhtolt. 82 leaves (9 5⁄8 x 7 1⁄8 in.; 245 x 182 mm.). 16 full-page and 3 smaller miniatures, 3 decorated incipit pages, and numerous illuminated initials. Purchased on the Lewis Cass Ledyard Fund, 1933.*

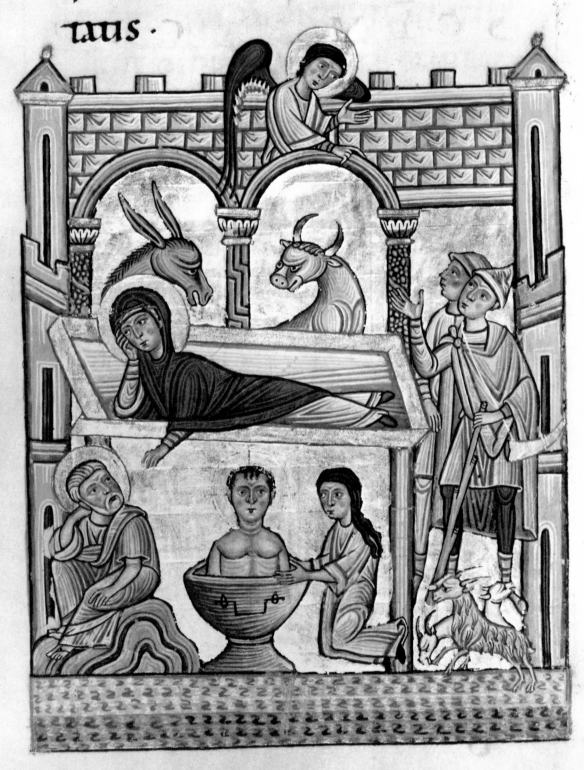

12

ST. MATTHEW THE EVANGELIST, ST. MARK THE EVANGELIST

England, about 1130 [*M. 777, fols. 3v, 24v*]

Each of the Gospels in this manuscript is preceded by a full-page miniature representing an evangelist seated upon his symbol, an iconographic feature apparently unique at this early date. The origin of this iconography is obscure, but at least two derivations have been suggested: one from oriental planet representations where the planet divinities ride or sit upon their zodiacal signs, and the other from western representations of the four elements riding upon animal symbols. The latter derivation requires the equation of the elements with the evangelists, an association with both literary and artistic parallels. The two evangelists shown here are Matthew, with the angel, and Mark, with the lion. The miniatures appear archaic for the period, and exhibit a kind of broadened school of Reims style which may well depend upon some Carolingian model. A sixteenth-century owner, Stephen Batman (d. 1584), has inscribed his name, in pseudo Anglo-Saxon characters, on the scroll held by Mark. Batman had helped Matthew Parker, the Archbishop of Canterbury, to assemble the great collection of books and manuscripts which he bestowed upon Corpus Christi College in Cambridge.

GOSPELS, *in Latin. England; about 1130. 76 leaves (10 ⅜ x 6 ¾ in.; 264 x 172 mm.). 4 full-page miniatures, 8 decorated initials. Purchased on the Lewis Cass Ledyard Fund, 1932.*

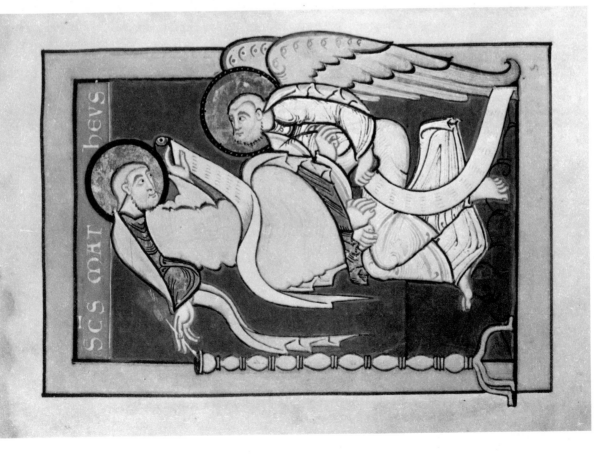

13

CORONATION OF ST. EDMUND

England, second quarter of the XII century [*M.736, fol. 8v*]

The Coronation of St. Edmund and the thirty-one other full-page miniatures devoted to his life form the longest and most important Edmund cycle antedating the fifteenth century. This cycle and the accompanying texts, which relate the saint's life, passion, and miracles, make up one of the earliest illustrated biographies of an English saint that has been preserved. Almost all of the miniatures in the cycle depict events described in the passion text of Abbo of Fleury (945–1004). The rest, all miracles, are based on a late and eclectic miracle text ascribed to Osbert of Clare, who evidently composed it at the request of Abbot Anselm sometime before the execution of this manuscript. The full-page miniatures, among the finest English productions of the century, have been attributed to the Alexis Master, who is credited with the founding of the St. Albans school of painting. This master, who received his name from the St. Alexis cycle in the St. Albans Psalter now in Hildesheim (church of St. Godehard), seems to have specialized in the creation of great narrative cycles. Such manuscripts as this, which were commissioned by abbeys in honor of their patron saints, were regarded as monuments to the saint and abbey alike.

LIFE, PASSION, AND MIRACLES OF ST. EDMUND, KING AND MARTYR, *in Latin. England, probably for the Abbey of Bury St. Edmunds; during the abbacy of Anselm in the second quarter of the XII century. 100 leaves (10¾ x 7¼ in.; 274 x 187 mm.). 32 full-page miniatures, 12 historiated and 27 large illuminated initials. Purchased in 1927.*

14

DEPOSITION AND ENTOMBMENT, PENTECOST

Belgium, middle of the XII century [*M.883, fols. 51v, 62v*]

At the time this manuscript was produced in the region of the Meuse river, the arts of stained glass, enamel work, and metal work also flourished. Artists were frequently accomplished in several media, resulting in the intermingling of figural and ornamental styles. The borders of the robes in this Deposition, for example, have their exact counterparts on the Library's famous True Cross Triptych from the monastery of Stavelot, which was made in the 1150s. The Deposition, unlike later representations where the intent is to display the body of Christ (see our number 34, for example), emphasizes the activity of Joseph of Arimathea and Nicodemus, who remove the body from the cross. Below, Christ's face seems to show through the shroud. In the Pentecost the apostles are huddled on either side of Peter, who holds his keys. The Lectionary, which contains the Gospel and Epistle readings for the church year, is closely related to a *Collationes* of Johannes Cassianus made for the abbey of St. Trond, now in the University Library of Liège (Ms.230D).

LECTIONARY, *perhaps for the use of St. Trond, in Latin. Belgium; middle of the* XII *century. 247 leaves (6½ x 4 in.; 165 x 102 mm.). 3 full-page, 3 half-page, and 1 smaller miniature, 3 historiated initials, numerous illuminated initials. Purchased in part on the Belle da Costa Greene Fund, 1957.*

15

ST. MARK THE EVANGELIST

Constantinople, XII century [M.692, fol. 123v]

The arrangement of the text in this Lectionary (which here contains readings from the Gospels) and Menology (with readings from the lives of the saints) is unusual because it is disposed in the shape of a cross. While some leaves with this cruciform arrangement can be found in Greek manuscripts, complete codices are far rarer. A notable and early example of the latter is a small ninth-century Greek Gospels in Princeton (University Library, Garrett Ms.1). More nearly contemporary with our manuscript are two Lectionaries in London (British Museum, Add.Ms.39603) and Washington (Dumbarton Oaks, Ms.1), the latter of which had adopted the cruciform text after a third of the book had already been written in two columns. A Gospels in Paris (Bibliothèque Nationale, grec.64), which has a number of cruciform text pages, also has some stylistic connections with the present manuscript. Of the four evangelist portraits usually found in such manuscripts only two have been preserved, those of Mark, illustrated here, and John. Both of these conform to well-established Byzantine types and are not actual portraits. Mark, for example, is depicted as a dark-haired, bearded, and swarthy young man. On his lectern is an open book containing the beginning of his Gospel, while that on his lap contains the first Gospel reading that follows (Mark:II:23). This portrait, complete with its array of writing implements, is close in style and detail to one in another twelfth-century Gospels in Paris (Bibliothèque Nationale, grec.189). In addition to the customary evangelist portraits, this Lectionary also contains a large number of marginal scenes, some unfinished, which resemble those found in contemporary monastic Psalters.

LECTIONARY OF THE GOSPELS, *in Greek, with cruciform text throughout. Constantinople or a dependant scriptorium;* XII *century. 293 leaves (13 ⅛ x 9 ⅛ in.; 335 x 233 mm.). 2 evangelist portraits, 4 decorated title pages, 34 pages with marginal scenes. Purchased in 1925.*

16

TRINITY AND THE CREATION OF THE WORLD

England, about 1215–1220 [*M.791, fol. 4v*]

The Lothian Bible, so named because the volume was once part of the Marquis of Lothian's library at Blickling Hall, is a virtual compendium of Biblical illustration where many books are introduced by multiscene historiated initials. That for such a rarely illustrated book as Esther, for example, receives nine scenes. Some of these initials have been painted on separate but smoother pieces of vellum inserted prior to illumination, a procedure used to achieve a painting surface finer than that provided by the manuscript itself. The miniatures are stylistically related to the Huntingfield Psalter, also in the Morgan Library (M.43), and share some iconographic details with a somewhat later Psalter in Oxford (New College, Ms.322), which has been attributed, in part, to W. de Brailes. While some Bibles, such as the twelfth-century Bury Bible in Cambridge (Corpus Christi College, Ms.2), have lost their frontispieces, this manuscript has not. An iconographical rarity, it shows the Trinity and the Creation of the World. At the top a Trinity of the unusual type where Christ's standing body seems joined to that of the Father is flanked by nine choirs of angels. In the center are the Dove of the Holy Spirit moving over the abyss; the fallen angels, who evidently formed one of the ten choirs and occupied the now blank register above; and the four rivers of Paradise of Genesis (II: 10–14). The six roundels at the bottom depict scenes from the Creation of the Angels to Eve.

BIBLE, *in Latin. Abbey of St. Albans, England; about 1215–1220. 395 leaves (18¾ x 13 in.; 476 x 330 mm.). 1 frontispiece, 8 very large, 45 large, and 13 small historiated initials. 4 very large and numerous smaller illuminated initials. 11 initials have been removed, some historiated. Gift of Mr. Philip Hofer, 1935.*

17

SIX SCENES FROM THE LIFE OF CHRIST

England, third quarter of the XIII century [*M.756, fol. 8*]

The Cuerden Psalter, named after a nineteenth-century owner's library at Cuerden Hall (that of Robert Townley Parker), is the most richly illuminated of a group of three manuscripts all produced at the same time and place. The other two, both in the British Museum, are the Bible of William of Devon (Royal Ms.I.D.i.), named after its scribe, and a smaller Book of Hours attributed to the same hand (Egerton Ms.1151). While Canterbury, or its environs, has been proposed as the center of production, the reasons for doing so are insufficient. Clearly, however, the center was a sophisticated one, and evidently in direct contact with the most progressive French illumination of the day. The faces and garments of the graceful figures exhibit the flat linear drawing style practiced in France under St. Louis. A series of seven composite miniatures and a full-page miniature—one of the earliest examples of a crowned *Virgo lactans* in a manuscript— precede the Psalter. The third of the composite miniatures, shown here, depicts the Crucifixion, Descent from the Cross, Resurrection, Holy Women at the Sepulchre, Noli Me Tangere, and the Incredulity of Thomas.

PSALTER, *with Calendar for Sarum use, in Latin. England, perhaps in the vicinity of Canterbury; third quarter of the* XIII *century. 241 leaves (11½ x 7¾ in.; 293 x 198 mm.). 1 full-page miniature, 7 full-page composite miniatures, 23 calendar medallions (one excised), 8 large and 178 smaller historiated initials, many marginal grotesques and hunting scenes. Purchased in 1929.*

18

YOLANDE DE SOISSONS KNEELING BEFORE A STATUE OF THE VIRGIN, HOLY FACE OF CHRIST

France, about 1290 [M.729, fol. 232v, 15]

This unusually refined and luxuriously illustrated Psalter–Book of Hours was produced about 1290, in Northern France, probably in the vicinity of Amiens, for the noble lady who is shown here kneeling before a statue of the Virgin and Child. On the basis of the arms in this border and elsewhere, she has been identified as Yolande de Soissons (born about 1241), Dame de Coeuvres, Vicomtesse de Soissons, who was married about 1265 to Bernard V, Sire de Moreuil (flourished 1259–1302). This miniature occurs at the beginning of the first Hour of the Virgin, Matins. Unlike the following Psalter–Book of Hours (number 19), also an early example of the type, the illustrations for the Hours are on a par—both in size and importance—with those of the Psalter portion. The illustrations are by at least two North French artists, the more refined of whom was familiar with English manuscripts and worked in a style similar to that of Maître Honoré. It was he who painted the powerful head of Christ shown here, which follows the prayer to St. Veronica and resembles a sudarium type found in earlier English manuscripts. Sometime before 1830 these two miniatures and eighteen others were removed from the manuscript. These and the codex curiously came up at the same W. Y. Ottley sale in London (1838), where Sir Frederic Madden recognized their relationship. Shortly thereafter, because of the unusual iconography of the miniatures, the manuscript was misbound. While some of these errors have been corrected, problems concerning the original order of the manuscript still remain. The manner in which the excised leaves were relaid into the manuscript is clearly visible in those reproduced here. The Holy Face, which still retains its former folio number, has now been rebound at the beginning of the volume, where it illustrates the prayer to St. Veronica.

PSALTER AND BOOK OF HOURS, *possibly use of Amiens, in Latin and French. Northern France, probably in the vicinity of Amiens; about 1290; for Yolande de Soissons. 434 leaves (7⅛ x 5¼ in.; 182 x 134 mm.). 40 full-page miniatures, the last added about 1380 by an artist close to the Passion Master, 24 calendar scenes, 66 historiated initials, 2 added by the same hand as above, numerous illuminated initials, and full-page borders with scenes and grotesques. Purchased in 1927.*

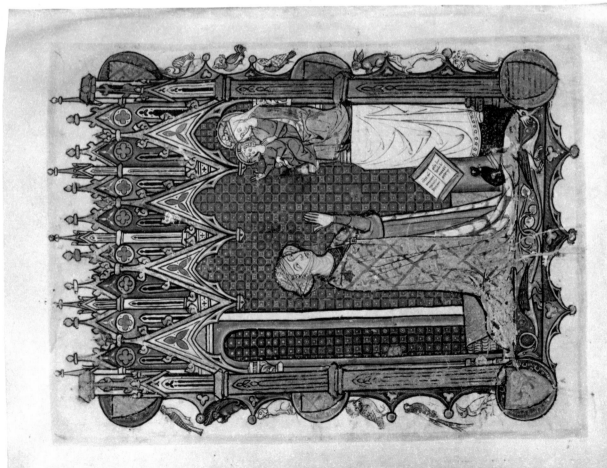

19

FOUR SCENES FROM THE STORY OF DAVID AND ABSALOM, EMPRESS CATHERINE DE COURTENAY CROWNED BY THE VIRGIN

France, last quarter of the XIII century, the first partially repainted by an Italian artist of the XIV century [M.730, fols. 127v, 214]

Before the Book of Hours became popular as an independent volume, some of its main texts, such as the Hours of the Virgin and the Office of the Dead, were frequently attached to the Psalter, as in this manuscript. The miniatures of these additions, however, are not as impressive as those of the Psalter, which contains more than the usual cycle of illustrations. Besides the prefatory cycle of eighteen multiscene miniatures covering the Creation of the World to the Coronation of the Virgin, there are large multiscene initials and full-page miniatures marking the eight divisions of the Psalter itself. Each of the eight groups of scenes, which chronologically illustrate the life of David, is preceded by an explanatory text in French. Shown here is the second of four miniatures found before the last division (Psalm CIX), which contains the following scenes: David's army at the Jordan, the division of his army into three parts, his battle with Absalom, and Joab killing Absalom. While no other work by this skillful portrayer of dramatic action is known, a Psalter in Vienna (Nationalbibliothek, Ms.ser.nov.2611) has similar decorative features. The original owners of this codex, according to heraldic evidence, were Ghuiluys de Boisleux and her husband Jean de Neuville-Vitasse. Through the latter's connection with the Courtenays, the manuscript descended to Catherine de Courtenay, the Empress of Constantinople (d. 1308). It was she who ordered an Italian artist to repaint two miniatures with representations of herself and her family. In the one shown here, illustrating the first Hour of the Virgin, she is crowned by the Virgin.

PSALTER AND BOOK OF HOURS, *use of Arras, in Latin and French. Northeastern France, probably Arras; last quarter of the XIII century. 251 leaves (7¾ x 5¾ in.; 197 x 147 mm.). 31 full-page miniatures, all but two with compartments, 24 calendar illustrations, 3 calendrical charts, 11 large historiated initials, and numerous large and small illuminated initials, some with figures. Purchased in 1927.*

20

NATIVITY AND ANNUNCIATION TO THE SHEPHERDS

Germany, between 1200 and 1232 [*M.710, fol. 16v*]

The Berthold Missal, which takes its name from the Abbot of Weingarten who commissioned it between 1200 and 1232, is without question the masterpiece of the Weingarten school of painting, quite possibly the finest and most luxurious thirteenth-century manuscript produced in Germany, and certainly a major monument of Romanesque art. Most of its miniatures, including the Nativity reproduced here, are by an exceptionally forceful and expressive artist who has been named the Master of the Berthold Missal after this, his masterpiece. The same artist also illuminated a manuscript containing fourteen Old Testament Prophets and Lives of the Saints which is now divided between the Public Libraries of Leningrad (Ms.lat.F.v.I.133) and New York (Spencer Ms.1). The manuscript still retains its original jewelled cover, a masterpiece of German goldsmiths' work. A small statue of the Virgin and Child occupies the center, indicating the importance of her cult at Weingarten (see also the following entry). Surrounding the statue are the four evangelists, the archangels Michael and Gabriel, the virtues Virginity and Humility (ascribed to the Virgin by St. Bernard, whose works were preserved at the abbey), Saints Oswald and Martin (the abbey's patron saints), Abbot Berthold (donor), and Saint Nicholas. The Library, in 1943, published a monograph on the Berthold Missal and its cover by Hanns Swarzenski.

MISSAL, *use of Weingarten Abbey, in Latin. Weingarten Abbey, Swabia, Germany; illuminated between 1200 and 1232 by the Master of the Berthold Missal for Abbot Berthold of Haimburg. 165 leaves (11 ½ x 8 in.; 293 x 204 mm.). 21 full-page, 5 half-page, and 2 smaller miniatures, 6 full-page illuminated texts, 19 historiated and numerous large and small illuminated initials. Purchased in 1926.*

21

CORONATION OF THE VIRGIN

Germany, early XIII century [M.711, fol. 57]

This volume, a sister manuscript of the Berthold Missal (our preceding entry), was evidently commissioned by Hainricus Sacrista, since his name and portrait occur several times in the manuscript. While a number of monks of this name are, in fact, mentioned in Weingarten records during the late twelfth and early thirteenth centuries, there is no agreement as to which our Hainricus is (or if he is one) or whether his manuscript was made before or after the more famous Berthold Missal. On stylistic grounds, however, the miniatures would appear to be later, for they are more gracious, delicate, and feminine—Gothic qualities not seen in the Berthold group, which exhibits a more Romanesque intensity and robustness. Two other stylistically related manuscripts, both in the Public Library of Fulda (Mss.Aa.32, Aa.40), are by miniaturists who have been regarded as followers of the Master of the Berthold Missal. The Virgin was especially honored at Weingarten, and this miniature of her Coronation precedes the Canon of the Mass. The same type of Coronation, but with Hainricus instead of the evangelists' symbols and the rivers of Paradise, is rendered in relief on the cover of the manuscript. Both this manuscript and the Berthold Missal remained in Weingarten Abbey until its secularization early in the nineteenth century.

GRADUAL, SEQUENTIARY, AND SACRAMENTARY, *use of Weingarten Abbey, in Latin. Weingarten Abbey, Swabia, Germany; early* XIII *century; for Hainricus Sacrista. 147 leaves (9½ x 6¾ in.; 242 x 172 mm.). 5 full-page miniatures, 24 calendar medallions, 35 historiated initials, 2 illuminated text pages, 1 unfinished page with elaborate border, and numerous small illuminated initials. Purchased in 1926.*

22

VIRGIN AND CHILD ENTHRONED WITH HEINRICUS PRESPITER AND LADY CHUNEGUNDIS

Austria, middle of the XIII century [*M.808, fol. 29v*]

This Gospels is one of the best examples of the art of Austria during its transition from the Romanesque to the Gothic periods. Its most important miniatures are not its evangelist portraits, however, but portraits of four individuals that provide evidence for the dating and localization of the codex: Gerungus of Weistrach and Yda, presumably his wife, who were patrons of Seitenstetten Abbey; Heinricus Prespiter, who has been identified as Heinricus I, the abbot of Seitenstetten from 1247 to 1250; and Chunegundis, an otherwise unknown patroness. The last two are in the dedication miniature, reproduced here, where they present the book to the Virgin, the patroness of the abbey. Their faces are almost identical—portrait features were lacking during this period—and were it not for the marginal inscriptions their identification would not have been possible. Chunegundis and Gerungus may have contributed toward the cost of the book as well as to the abbey. A number of details, especially in the evangelist portraits, were copied from a late twelfth-century Gospels at Vorau (Chorherrenstift, Ms.346). The script, boldly and beautifully executed, seems to justify the scribe's colophon: "He who finished me, hey, how well he could write." The Seitenstetten Gospels, as well as our number 23, also a thirteenth-century Seitenstetten manuscript, remained in the abbey library (where they were designated as Cod. XV and XIV respectively) until the present century.

GOSPELS, *in Latin. Austria, probably in the Benedictine monastery of Seitenstetten; middle of the* XIII *century. 240 leaves (12 x 8 in.; 305 x 204 mm.). 6 full-page and 2 smaller miniatures, 10 decorated canon tables, 4 historiated initials, and other large illuminated initials. Purchased in 1940.*

23

VIRGIN AND CHILD ENTHRONED

Austria, second half of the XIII century [*M.855, fol. 110v*]

Although this manuscript is generally designated as a Missal, it is not. While some of the requisite texts, such as the Gradual, Sequentiary, and Sacramentary are present, though not liturgically integrated, others are lacking, such as the lessons from the Gospels and Epistles. Its rather meagre calendar does contain, however, two important entries which localize the manuscript in the Benedictine monastery of Seitenstetten; the name of its founder, Udalschalk von Stille (May 11), and its dedication date (November 3). Of the three full-page miniatures in this codex, the two most important precede the Canon of the Mass, face each other, and are by an Italian miniaturist who was strongly influenced by the style associated with a manuscript written by Giovanni da Gaibana, an Epistolary of 1259 in the cathedral of Padua (Biblioteca Capitolare). They represent the enthroned Virgin nursing her Child (shown here) and the Crucifixion. The donor or maker of the manuscript, perhaps an abbot of the monastery of Our Lady of Seitenstetten, may be shown as the small figure who kneels before the Virgin's throne. The gold background of the miniature is richly burnished, as are those of the historiated initials, which were executed by local Austrians and which represent subjects that are appropriate for the feasts they illustrate.

GRADUAL, SEQUENTIARY, AND SACRAMENTARY, *use of Seitenstetten, in Latin. Seitenstetten Abbey, Austria; second half of the* XIII *century. 220 leaves (12 ¾ x 9 in.; 322 x 228 mm.). 12 calendar illustrations, 3 full-page miniatures, 50 historiated initials, and numerous illuminated initials. Purchased with the assistance of the Fellows, 1951.*

24

SIX OLD TESTAMENT SCENES

Bohemia, first quarter of the XIII century [*M.739, fol. 11v*]

This Book of Hours, entitled *Cursus Sanctae Mariae*, is a very early example of the independent text, which, unlike the two Books of Hours previously discussed (our numbers 18 and 19) is not attached to a Psalter. Like those volumes, however, the text is preceded by a large cycle of miniatures. In this case there are thirty-two full pages of miniatures which depict, in chronological sequence, scenes from the Creation to Pentecost. Each is supplied with inscriptions in German. The example shown here is divided into three registers depicting the drunken Lot and his daughter's deception, Isaac bearing the wood of his sacrifice and the substitution of the ram as Abraham's victim, the birth of Jacob and Esau (meaning hairy), and Esau bringing a rabbit to Isaac and Rebecca. This miniature, actually a pen drawing in red and sepia against a background of colored bands, is by the best of the three artists who worked on the manuscript. Both his style and iconography show a relationship to the frescoes in the Chapel of St. Katherine at Znaim, near Luka. The calendar of this manuscript is of exceptional historical interest, for it contains a wealth of obituary notices relating to various saints, nuns, bishops, and the royalty of Bohemia, and more specifically, to Prague and the monasteries of Treibnitz and Znaim. On the basis of this calendrical and other evidence, it has been suggested that the first owner of the book was the then Margravine Kunegund of Moravia, from whom the manuscript then descended to her niece, St. Agnes of Bohemia. In 1937 the Library published *Cursus Sanctae Mariae*, a monograph on the manuscript by Meta Harrsen, who was a former keeper of manuscripts at the Library.

BOOK OF HOURS, *for Premonstratensian use, in Latin and German. Bohemia, probably in the monastery of Luka, near Znaim; first quarter of the XIII century. 183 leaves (11 x 7¾ in.; 280 x 197 mm.). 32 full-page miniatures (all in 3 registers except 1, which has 2) and 8 smaller ones, 12 historiated initials, 7 large decorated initials and numerous smaller ones with figures and animals. Purchased in 1928.*

Do chom loth in einen wart dar was
man noch wib was. do sprachen sine
tochtere. wir sulin unsern vart trunchen

ysaac. Diz ist san sat abraha. vnde get uf den synay sinen sun opfern berch

Eine burdin holzes tret uf im

vn lit in chindel bette   Diz ist ysaac vn rebecca. Diz

Diz ist rebecca vn ysaachel sorb

Diz ist iacob vn esav.

25

ARCHANGEL MICHAEL WEIGHING A SOUL

England, second quarter of the XIV century [M.700, fol. 2]

This rather large and extensive Book of Hours was made for Lady Hawisia de Bois, who is several times herein named and depicted, usually with her husband and sister. Aside from her identification with an Avicia de Boys, mentioned in a deed of 21 May 1328, little else about her is known except that her family seems to have been connected with Buckinghamshire. The miniatures, rendered in a rather flat and dry drawing style, closely resemble those in another English Horae in the Escorial (Ms.Q.II.6). Some of the miniatures in the Treatise of Walter de Milemete in Oxford (Christ Church Library, Ms.E.11), which was presented to Edward III about 1326–1327, share the same tendency toward awkwardness in the drawing. At the beginning of the book are two full-page miniatures of the archangels Gabriel and Michael, the latter of which, reproduced here, weighs a soul. While there seem to be no early direct literary sources for Michael as soul weigher —he is a kind of later-day Anubis, who weighed the heart in Egyptian funerary art— the scales, long an attribute of justice, may refer to his roles in judgment and as a protector of souls. A malformed devil pulls on the cup containing the soul so that it might outweigh the devil in the other. The couple flanking Michael wear the de Bois colors and probably represent Hawisia and her husband, whose arms adorn the border.

BOOK OF HOURS, *use of Sarum, in Latin and French. England; second quarter of the* XIV *century; for Lady Hawisia de Bois. 198 leaves (12½ x 8½ in.; 318 x 216 mm.). 4 full-page miniatures, 24 calendar medallions, 41 large and 3 small historiated initials, borders on every page, many with grotesques and arms. Purchased in 1929.*

26

CANON TABLE

Armenia, 1274 [M.740, fol. 4v]

According to its colophon, this Gospels was made in 1274 for Marshal Oshin, Lord of Lambron, in Sis, the capital of Cilicia. Its text, which is divided into lessons in accordance with Armenian custom, has lost all but one of its evangelist portraits, that of John, who is shown dictating his Gospel to the scribe Prochoros. No example with Prochoros is known before the tenth century, and the type may have been invented as a frontispiece for Symeon Metaphrastes' late tenth-century hagiographical work, which included the life of St. John. While two of the missing portraits have been found in Cambridge (Fitzwilliam Museum, McClean Ms.201), that of Luke, perhaps concealed in some scrapbook of cuttings, has yet to be discovered. In addition to evangelist portraits, many mediaeval Gospels were also supplied with Eusebian canon tables, which were named after their inventor, Eusebius of Caesarea (about 265–340). It is in these canon tables, which show in what passages each Gospel agreed or differed from the others, that the most unusual decorative feature of this manuscript is found: the apparently unprecedented (and unexplained) strange nude figures with long hair and tails. The other naturalistic and stylized floral and animal forms on the page shown here have been part of the standard Armenian repertory since the tenth century and find parallels, for example, in the nearly contemporary Royal Gospels of Queen Keran in Jerusalem (Library of the Armenian Patriarchate, Ms.2563), made two years earlier.

GOSPELS, *in Armenian. Sis, Cilicia; 1274; written by the scribe Constantin for Marshal Oshin, Lord of Lambron. 320 leaves (10¾ x 7⅛ in.; 273 x 200 mm.). 1 full-page miniature, 4 decorated canon tables, 6 decorated pages. Purchased in 1928.*

27

CRUCIFIXION

Ethiopia, 1400–1401 [*M.828, fol. 14*]

This Crucifixion and the twenty-five other full-page miniatures in this manuscript are important not only because of their early date, but also because of their unusual iconography. Indeed, few older illuminated Gospels from Ethiopia survive, and the Haiq Gospels (Addis Ababa, National Library, Ms.A.5), the oldest illuminated Ethiopian manuscript known, was made before 1350. While this Crucifixion is unusual in that Christ is not represented, it is not unique, for this feature also occurs in the earlier Ethiopian Gospels of Kuskam Monastery now in Paris (Bibliothèque Nationale, eth.32). The miniature contains the following inscriptions: "The sun and the moon, how they became blood. Soul of the thief on the right, how the angel of light brought it forth and covered it with his wings (viewer's left). The angel of darkness, how he brought forth the soul of the thief on the left (viewer's right). His side was pierced with a spear. He is given to drink, on a reed myrrh mingled with gall." The artist has apparently made an error, for both figures flanking the cross hold spears.

GOSPELS, *in Ethiopic. Ethiopia; during the year 29 August 1400 – 28 August 1401; for Princess Zir Gānēlā, granddaughter of King Amda Seyon. 207 leaves (14¼ x 9⅞ in.; 362 x 251 mm.). 26 full-page miniatures by two artists, 8 decorated canon tables, 4 incipit pages. Purchased on the Lewis Cass Ledyard Fund, 1948.*

ፀሐይ፡ወወርኅ፡ዘከመ፡ኮኑ፡ደመ፡

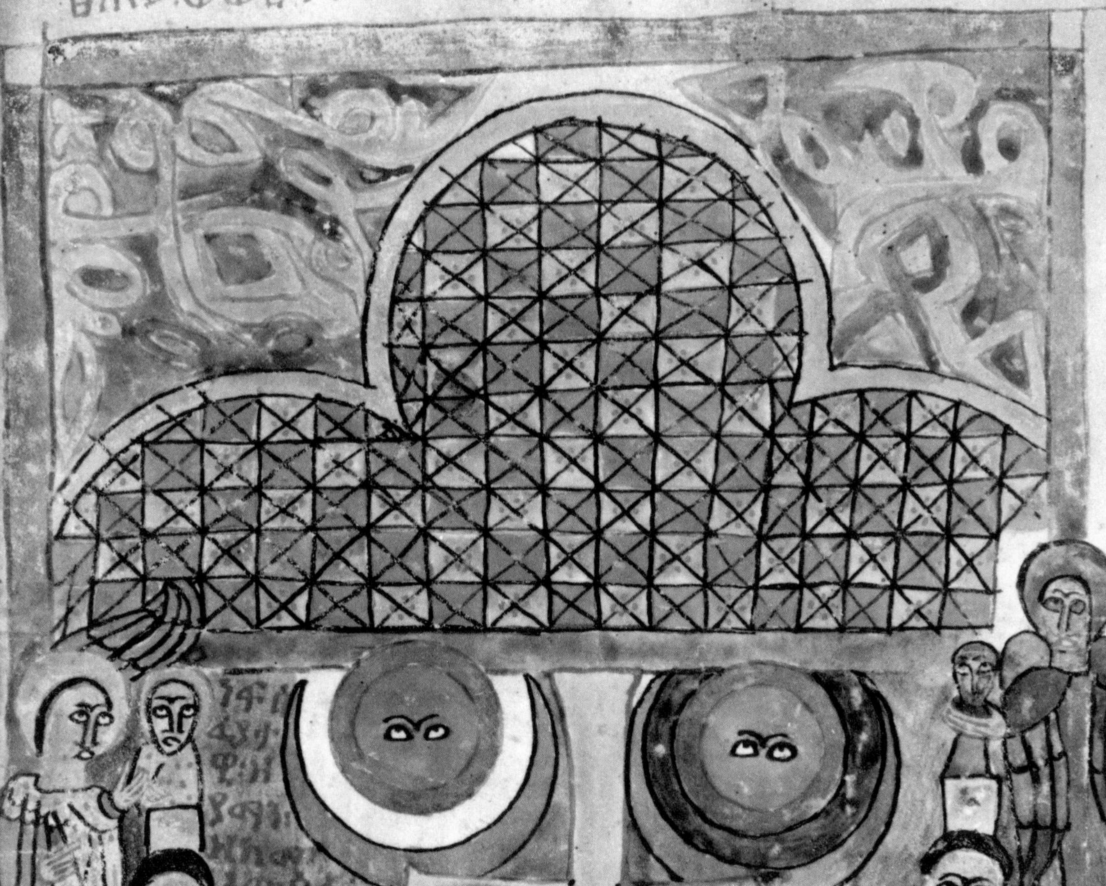

28

THE FIRST KISS OF LANCELOT AND GUINEVERE, LANCELOT RESCUES GUINEVERE BY CROSSING THE SWORD BRIDGE

France, early XIV century [*M.805, fol. 67; M.806, fol. 166*]

Between the years 1275 and 1330 Arthurian manuscripts were at the height of their popularity, and many illustrated cycles were produced. The finest and most important depicting the Lancelot legend is this manuscript, which was made in northeastern France, perhaps at Amiens, at the beginning of the fourteenth century. The story of Lancelot, one of the most famous knights of King Arthur's Round Table, became especially important when Chrétien de Troyes (about 1170)—on whose work the Lancelot poem is partly based—transformed him into the chivalric lover of Queen Guinevere. Shown here is the first kiss of Lancelot and Guinevere, who are accompanied by Galehot (Sir Galahad), the arranger of the meeting. On the right-hand part of the miniature Senechal converses with the Lady of Malohaut and Laura of Carduel. The first kiss, here given its finest mediaeval representation, was immortalized in Dante's *Divine Comedy* (Inferno v.127–138). The narrative quality of the miniatures and their strict adherence to the text is also seen in the second miniature reproduced, which illustrates one of the many episodes where Lancelot proved his love by rescuing Guinevere from her captors. In this case Meleagant, the wicked son of King Baudemagus, had held Guinevere prisoner in a tower guarded by lions. The tower, located on the other side of a raging river, was bridged by a sharp sword that would cut those who attempted to cross it. Lancelot, although covered with armor and chain mail, nevertheless bleeds as he successfully crosses the bridge. Later he is met by King Baudemagus, who, with Guinevere, had just witnessed the ordeal from the tower. These large miniatures and some of the historiated initials are the work of an artist whose style appears in Roger of Salerno's Medical Treatise in London (British Museum, Sloane Ms.1977) and in a life of St. Benedicta from Saint Quentin in Berlin (Staatliche Museen, Kupferstichkabinett, Ms.78.B.16). Most of the historiated initials are by an artist who may have worked on a *Somme le Roy* in Paris (Bibliothèque de l'Arsenal, Ms.6329).

LE ROMAN DE LANCELOT DU LAC, *in French. Northeastern France; beginning of the* XIV *century. 266 leaves in two volumes (13⅝ x 10 in.; 346 x 255 mm.).* M.805, I: *141 leaves, 18 oblong miniatures, 83 historiated initials* M.806, II: *125 leaves, 21 oblong miniatures, 54 historiated initials. A third volume (*M.807*), but of the* XV *century, completes the text and contains but one miniature. Purchased on the Lewis Cass Ledyard Fund, 1938.*

29

ASCENSION, CHRIST WASHING THE FEET OF THE APOSTLES

France, second quarter of the XIV century [*M.754, fols. 114, 51*]

It was only after the discovery of the first half of this fragmentary Book of Hours in the British Museum (Add.Ms.36684) that a localization based on the use of its Hours of the Virgin could be made, since that text was not in the Morgan portion. This manuscript and two other stylistically related Horae were all made for use in the diocese of Thérouanne, in northern France, where they were probably produced. The other two are in Marseilles (Bibliothèque Municipale, Ms.111) and Baltimore (Walters Art Gallery, w.90). Most of the miniatures are actually large historiated initials situated within many-spired architectural frames. The Ascension reproduced here, for example, occurs within the letter A of *Après*, the first word of the commemoration of the Ascension found at the beginning of the life of St. Margaret. Since the border of this and the other miniatures illustrating Margaret's life all contain a kneeling woman, it has been supposed that the book was made for a woman named Margaret. This conclusion must be discarded here, however, because the woman occurs in the border of almost every miniature, and the Margaret text is not unusual in manuscripts made for women because Margaret was the patron saint of childbirth. It is not without interest that on the opposite page the same kneeling woman is clearly pregnant. Christ Washing the Feet of the Apostles, within the letter C of *Converte*, is for the Compline text of an unusual cycle illustrating what the rubric calls the Hours of the Holy Sacrament of the Altar.

BOOK OF HOURS, *fragment, use of Thérouanne, in Latin. Life of St. Margaret, in French. Northeastern France, possibly Thérouanne; second quarter of the XIV century. 136 leaves (6⅛ x 4¾ in.; 156 x 111 mm.). 3 miniatures, 26 large historiated initials, numerous borders with scenes and grotesques. Purchased in 1929.*

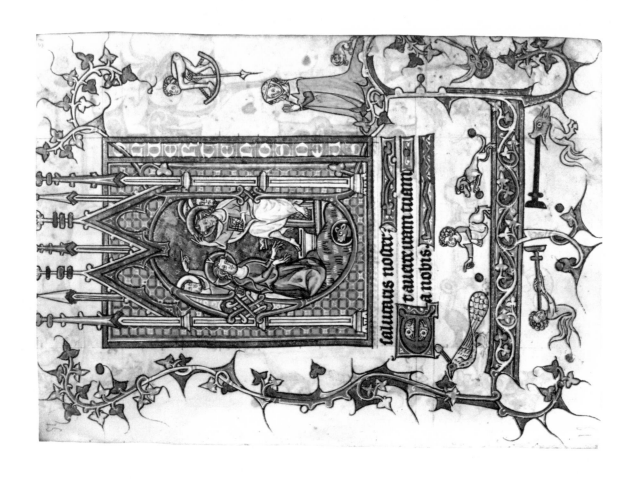

30

ZODIAC AND PLANETS ENCIRCLING THE EARTH

Austria, first quarter of the XV century [M.722, fol. 18]

This full-page diagram of the Zodiac also shows the irregular movements of the sun, moon, and planets around the earth. The variable paths of the sun, for example, are described by two circles, labelled *centrum deferentis* and *centrum equantis*, neither of whose centers, however, are located at the center of the earth, the *centrum mundi*. This miniature, identical with and executed in the same atelier as one in Berlin (former Staatsbibliothek Ms.germ.fol.479), is situated at the beginning of the second of the two astrological texts in this codex. The first is Konrad von Megenberg's (1309–1374) German translation of the *Sphaera mundi*, the principal work of John Holywood, the thirteenth-century English astronomer and mathematician known as Sacrobosco. The second text, by Abd-al-Aziz—the mediaeval form of his name was Alchabitius—is indicative of the role that the translation of scientific Arabic texts played in the development of astronomy in the middle ages. The German version of the second text represents the work of Arnold von Freiburg (about 1312), who used the earlier Latin translation of Johannes Hispalensis (first half of the XII century).

SACROBOSCO (*John Holywood*). *Sphaera mundi and* ALCHABITIUS. *Libellus isagogicus, both in German. Austria; first quarter of the XV century. 48 leaves (12 x 9¼ in.; 305 x 235 mm.). 1 full-page miniature, 10 other charts and diagrams, 5 illuminated initials, 1 border scene. Purchased in 1927.*

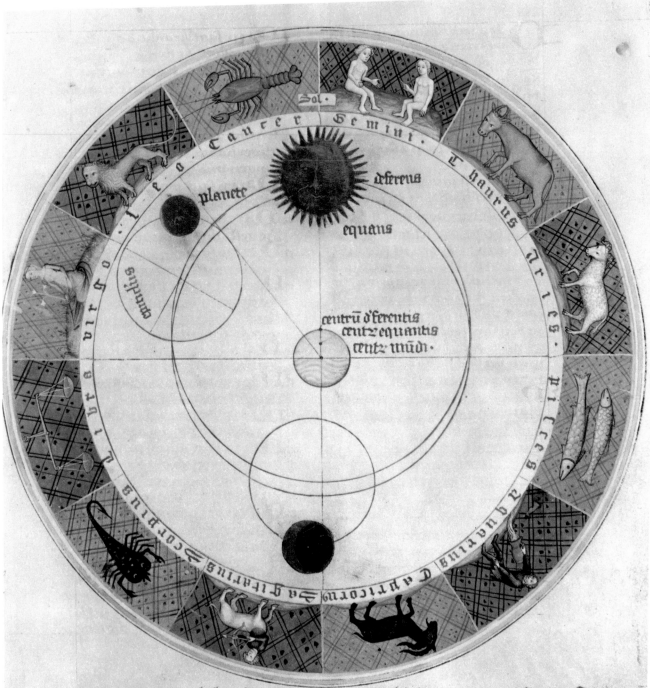

Dy figur der Epitikel der stende der richtunge der hindergeunge vnd der groſſteͦ
hoͤche aller planeten vnd des mones ſnellichait vnd treglichait ⸭

31

NIMROD BUILDING THE TOWER OF BABEL

Germany, about 1375–1380 [*M.769, fol. 28v*]

This profusely illustrated world chronicle, which treats events from the creation of the world to the death of Charlemagne, is called the *Christ-Herre Chronik* after its opening words, *Christ Herre Kaiser über aller Chraft....* While its text imitates the style of Rudolf von Ems—who left his own rhymed chronicle unfinished with the death of Solomon—it is actually an independent work which is more complete and richer in theological information. The work was commissioned by and dedicated to Landgraf Heinrich of Thuringia (1202–1247), a nephew of the Emperor Frederick the First. A *Christ-Herre* manuscript in Munich (Staatsbibliothek, Ms.germ.5) must have been made in the same workshop, for it is closely related in style and date. Illustrated here is Nimrod, whom Augustine, in his *City of God*, credits with the construction of the tower of Babel, describing him as a giant and as a "Hunter against the Lord."

ANONYMOUS IMITATOR OF RUDOLF VON EMS. *Christ-Herre Chronik, in German. South East Bavaria; about 1375–1380. 342 leaves (13 ½ x 9 ½ in.; 343 x 242 mm.). 243 large and smaller miniatures, 2 historiated initials, and 4 historiated borders. Purchased in 1931.*

Dez werckes sich besunden
an den sellen stunden
Vnd heten nider daz zil
der turnes gemacht als vil
Daz er sich gezoch
gen funf tausent schriten hoch

Vnd sibentzik vnd nawn hundr
vnd vier schrit am besunderr
Nit zwain vnd sibentzig ecken waz
der selb turn als ich er las
Van der geslacht nach der zal
waz auch als vil vber al
Alz ich hie gesprochen han
an har die schrift vnz chum getan
Daz funfzehen chinn schar
japhetes chinn gepar
Sem der ram gur man
siben vnd zwaintzig sin gewan
Er vnd mit im semew chinr
di hie vor genennet sint
Der iesleich ein geslacht liez
cham dreyzzig vater hiez
Der vrhab an im ward genomen
von de warn dreyzzig geslacht chomen
Der aller waz nach rehter zal
zway vnd sibentzig vber al
Die den turn wolten han
gemacht durch irn tumben wan
Biz daz got zu in sant
die potschaft die in ermant
Die vingen hochmart
der ir tumphait zu rat wart
O got wir vbermut ersach
er zurnt an si vnd sprach
In nit allem wlck chumt
an zung an sprach vnd an mumt
Da hin suln wir vnd daz erden
vnd die sprach also schenden
Daz ir chainem gezem
daz er des andn wort vernem
Vnd sein zungen niht versté
daz sammt sich do niht lenge mé
Er der wil got in warr zuhant
sprach vnd ir zung also geschant
Der vnd in deham dort
vstunt der chin sprach wort
Von ienem iz von disem hin
waz daz in allen vnder in
Des nam si michel wunder
iesleichs geslacht ret besunder
Ames ret vnserisch
daz ander rautzisch
Daz dritt iehaimisch ret
daz vierd tavrisch alda zu stet
Des funft der kriechisch
daz sechst haidmisch
Also het sich ir red vercherrt
alz si got selb het gelerrt

32

CRUCIFIXION

Italy, second half of the XIV century [M.800, fol. 39v]

Among the fourteenth-century Bolognese illuminators known by name are Franco Bolognese—who is praised by Dante—and Niccolò di Giacomo di Nascimbene (about 1330–about 1402), better known as Niccolò da Bologna, who illuminated this manuscript, signing his name (as Nicolaus de Bononia) on its most important miniature, the Crucifixion reproduced here. Although a relatively large number of other signed works exist, such as a single leaf with a similar Crucifixion in the Cleveland Museum of Art (Ms.24.1013), these are not dated, making it difficult to establish a firm chronology. Nevertheless, it has been suggested that the type of black background with scrolls used in this Crucifixion was characteristic for his middle period. The text of the manuscript, sometimes erroneously referred to as a Missal, is actually an Ordinal, which contains the rubricated directions and prayers for the preparation of the Mass and Canon. The Crucifixion accompanies the portion of the text dealing with the Canon of the Mass. In the fifteenth century a Benedictional, entitled *Benedictiones Episcopales*, was added.

ORDINAL, *in Latin. Bologna, Italy; second half of the* XIV *century; illuminated by Niccolò da Bologna. 76 leaves (9 x 6¼ in.; 228 x 160 mm.). 1 full-page miniature and 18 historiated initials. Purchased in 1937.*

33

NATIVITY AND ANNUNCIATION TO THE SHEPHERDS

Italy, second quarter of the XIV century [M.713, fol. 55]

This historiated initial C (of *Communicantes*)—a Nativity with the Holy Spirit descending on the Christ Child—and the Annunciation to the Shepherds in the lower border are by an anonymous artist thought to have been a pupil of Simone Martini, the Master of the St. George Codex. The artist is named after a St. George and the Dragon miniature (often compared with Martini's destroyed fresco in Avignon) in a Missal made for Cardinal Jacopo de Stefaneschi which is now in St. Peter's, Rome (Archivio Capitolare, Ms.c.129, known as the Codex of St. George). The Nativity actually illustrates the Communicantes for Christmas, a section of the Canon of the Roman Mass named after its first word. The variable parts of the Christmas Mass are not included here, however, and must have been contained, with other sections of the Temporale, in other volumes of the Missal. Indeed, recent research indicates that the Codex of St. George itself may have been part of this multivolume Missal, since it includes only a small portion of the Sanctorale, none of which is included in the Morgan volume, which contains only the Common of the Mass and Votive Masses.

MISSAL FRAGMENT, *use of Rome, in Latin. Italy; second quarter of the XIV century; illuminated by the Master of the St. George Codex. 167 leaves (14¾ x 10 in.; 375 x 255 mm.). 3 full-length historiated initials and numerous smaller initials, 2 full historiated borders, and numerous illuminated borders. Purchased in 1927.*

In nāt dominī in fīa actione.
Ommunicantes
et noctem ul dian
sacratissimam cele
brantes. qua ud quo bir ma
ne intemerata uirginitas huic
mundo cordit saluatorem.
Sed et memoriam uenerantes.
In primis eiusdem gloriose
semperq; uirginis marie ge.
nitricis eiusdem dei et domi
ni nostri ihu xpi. Sed et bto
rum apostolorum. In epy
phania domini et per octam
in fīa actionem.

34

DEPOSITION

England, about 1430–1440 [*M.893, fol. 36v*]

While English manuscript illumination suffered a great decline throughout the course of the fifteenth century, and its artists increasingly looked to the Continent for inspiration and models, there were nevertheless a few outstanding manuscripts produced there, which, for the most part, were fairly free from Continental influence. One of these is the Warwick Hours, which was illuminated by two distinct artists, about 1430–1440, for Henry Beauchamp, the Duke of Warwick. While the Hours of the Virgin are generally illustrated with scenes from the life of Mary, a passion cycle may sometimes be substituted. Such is the case in this manuscript, where the text for Vespers, which here also includes a memorial on the passion (as do the other hours), is introduced by the Deposition rather than the customary Flight into Egypt. This Deposition, which is surrounded by typical border decoration of the period, is of interest as an early example of the type which displays the body of Christ completely removed from the cross. (Numbers 10 and 14 in this book show the older type where the feet of Christ are still attached.) Two other miniatures in the passion series are also of iconographic interest, for they show the bloody sweat of Christ at Gethsemane, and the bloody footprints left by Christ on the way to Calvary. By 1482, to judge by the added table of golden numbers for the years 1482 to 1509, the manuscript reached Italy, where more texts and miniatures were added by North Italian artists. While these added miniatures are clearly Italian, the degree to which the writing and some of the initials imitate those in the English part is remarkable.

BOOK OF HOURS AND PSALTER, *use of Sarum, in Latin. England; about 1430–1440; for Henry Beauchamp, Duke of Warwick; with Italian additions of about 1482. 261 leaves (10¾ x 7⅜ in.; 273 x 188 mm.). 22 English and 5 North Italian half-page miniatures with fully decorated borders. Purchased on the Belle da Costa Greene Fund, with the assistance of the Fellows, and the special assistance of the Hon. Robert Woods Bliss, Mrs. W. Murray Crane, Mr. Childs Frick, Mr. William S. Glazier, Mrs. Matilda Geddings Gray, Mr. Arthur A. Houghton, Jr., Mr. and Mrs. Donald F. Hyde, Mr. Milton McGreevy, Colonel David McC. McKell, Mr. Joseph V. Reed, Mrs. Landon K. Thorne, Mr. Ralph Walker, Mr. Christian A. Zabriskie, and an anonymous foundation, 1958.*

Eus in adiutorium
meum intende Do
mine ad adiuuandu
me festina Gloria pri.
Sicut erat. Alleluya.
Ant Post partum. Ps
Etatus sum in hijs que dicta sunt
michi: in domū domini ibimus.
Stantes erant pedes nri. in atrijs tuis
ierusalem Ierusalen que edificatur ut
ciuitas: cuius participacio eius in idipm

35

MAN ARMED FOR FIGHTING ON FOOT

England, middle of the XV century [*M.775, fol. 122v*]

This collection of miscellaneous texts, which includes some relating to chivalry, was written for Sir John Astley (d. 1486), who was prominent in the service of King Edward IV and was himself famed for feats of arms at tournaments and jousts. Representations of specific chivalric events are fairly rare and this manuscript includes at least three: Sir John Astley jousting with an unknown contestant; Astley in mounted combat with Pierre de Masse, in Paris (29 August 1438); and Astley in a foot fight, with axes, against Philip Boyle of Aragon, in Smithfield (30 January 1441/2). Shown here, however, is yet another rare miniature where a man is being prepared for foot battle in one of the small huts erected near the lists for the purpose. The miniature accompanies a text which reads: "How a man schall be armyd at his ese when he schal fighte on foote."

ORDINANCES OF ARMOURY, JOUSTING, SWORD AND AXE COMBAT AND CHIVALRY IN GENERAL, WITH OTHER MISCELLANEOUS TEXTS, *in English. England; middle of the* XV *century; for Sir John Astley. 320 leaves (9¾ x 6¾ in.; 248 x 172 mm.). 4 full-page and 5 smaller miniatures by several hands, some astrological tables and diagrams, and numerous illuminated borders and initials. Purchased in 1931.*

How a man schall be armyd at his ese
when he schal fighte on foote

He schal haue noo schurte vp on him but a
dowbelet of ffustean lynyd with satene cutte
full of hooles. the dowbelet muste be strongeli bounde
there the poyntis muste be sette aboute the greet of the
arme. and the b ste before and beshynde and the gussetis
of mayle muste be sowid vn to the dowbelet in
the bonghit of the arme. and vndir the arme the ar
mynge poyntis muste be made of fyne twyne suche
as men make stryngis for crossebowes and they

36

ST. LUKE THE EVANGELIST, LAMENTATION, VIRGIN ENTHRONED, ANNUNCIATION

France, third quarter of the XV century [M.834, fols. 15, 21, 25, 29]

Although no documentary evidence connects this small Book of Hours with Jean Fouquet, the most important French painter of his time, the high quality and style of its miniatures have caused some scholars to attribute a number of them to Fouquet himself. There is no doubt, however, that the manuscript is connected with his workshop, for a number of its miniatures, such as the Lamentation and Virgin Enthroned (both reproduced here) derive from his greatest masterpiece, the Hours of Étienne Chevalier, the dismembered remains of which are mostly in Chantilly (Musée Condé, Ms.71). The Lamentation and portrait of St. Luke (also shown here), as well as a large portion of its miniatures, have been attributed to Jean Colombe, Fouquet's outstanding student. A similar Luke in a Book of Hours formerly in the Loncle collection (sold at Hôtel Drouot, Paris, 17 June 1960, lot 14) has also been attributed to Colombe. Whereas the Lamentation and Virgin Enthroned illustrate prayers to the Virgin (the *Obsecro te* and *O intemerata*), the Luke accompanies a reading dealing with the Annunciation taken from his Gospel. Probably the finest and most original miniature in the manuscript is the Annunciation shown here, which illustrates the beginning (Matins) of its most important text, the Hours of the Virgin. Most consistently attributed to Fouquet, it has also recently been connected with an artist who painted the same subject in the Hours of Diane de Croy, which is now in the University Library of Reading, but which was formerly in the Ruskin Museum at Sheffield.

BOOK OF HOURS, *use of Rome, in Latin. France, probably Tours; third quarter of the* XV *century; illuminated in the workshop of Jean Fouquet (with miniatures attributed to Jean Colombe) for a member of the Laval-Loué family. 174 leaves (4 ¼ x 3 ⅛ in.; 108 x 80 mm.). 25 full-page miniatures, 24 calendar medallions. Purchased with the assistance of the Fellows, 1950.*

37

CRAINTE DE DIEU AND CONTRITION SPEAK TO L'ÂME DÉVOTE, FOUR VIRTUES NAIL L'ÂME DÉVOTE'S HEART TO A CROSS

France, third quarter of the XV century [M.705, fols. 10, 60]

In 1454, René, the King of Naples, Sicily, and Jerusalem, wrote the text which these miniatures illustrate—an allegorical dialogue between the soul inflamed by Divine Love (*L'Âme Dévote*) and the heart (*Coeur*) led astray by worldly vanities. Other dramatis personae, such as *Crainte de Dieu* (Fear of God) and *Parfaite Contrition*, are also introduced: they denounce the transitory value of worldly joys and pleasures and show that the soul can only attain peace and true happiness by its union with and complete obedience to God. The work is apparently based on Boethius' *On the Consolation of Philosophy*. The two scenes reproduced here show personifications of *Crainte de Dieu* and *Parfaite Contrition* speaking to *L'Âme Dévote*; and the four virtues (grace with a lance, faith, hope and love) crucifying the heart of *L'Âme Dévote*. At one time it was thought that King René illuminated his own manuscripts, but now it is believed that he was only the patron of artists who were active in his native Anjou. All of the miniatures in the present manuscript exhibit the figure style of the Anjou court except for the first, which shows René presenting a copy of the book to Jean Bernard, Archbishop of Tours, to whom the text was dedicated. A number of other illustrated copies of the work survive, some of which, such as that in Berlin (Staatliche Museen, Kupferstichkabinett, Ms.78.C5), evidently derive from the Morgan miniatures, which may themselves depend directly on René's original manuscript.

RENÉ D'ANJOU. *Le mortifiement de vaine plaisance ou Traité entre l'Âme Dévote et le Coeur plein de Vanité. France, perhaps Anjou; third quarter of the XV century. 70 leaves (7 x 5 in.; 178 x 128 mm.). 9 half-page miniatures, 1 decorated border. Purchased in 1926.*

reature espirituelle faite
et cree par la voulente diceluy
treshault z trespuissant souue

as les deux armes de par
ihesus sur se fust de la croix
misdrent le cuer ensendroit

38

DUKE WILHELM OF AUSTRIA

Austria, between 1403 and 1406 [M.853, fol. 1v]

This text, which has traditionally been ascribed to Thomas Aquinas, comprises the full office for the feast of Corpus Christi (Body of Christ). Its frontispiece, reproduced here, appropriately depicts Duke Wilhelm "the Affable" contemplating an image of the body of Christ known as the Man of Sorrows, which is located within an initial S on the opposite page. The Duke, who is kneeling out-of-doors on a homemade prie-dieu, holds a scroll with the words *Ave verum corpus Christi* (Hail, true body of Christ). On the ground is a shield with the colors of Austria; behind him stands his armed squire. The panel below contains five armorial shields: the large central one, which is that of the Duke's wife Johanna of Anjou, is surrounded by the arms of the provinces over which he ruled, Carinthia and Carniola on the left and Styria and Tyrol on the right. Since the Duke married Johanna in 1403 and died on 15 July 1406, as a result of a riding accident, the manuscript was probably executed between these dates. Nikolaus of Brünn, who was the Viennese court illuminator, painted two likenesses of the Duke, of which this one is the more important. The second, in a German translation of the *Rationale divinorum officiorum* of Gulielmus Durandis (Vienna, Nationalbibliothek, Ms.2765), shows the Duke and his wife kneeling before a Man of Sorrows triptych, a subject for which the Duke apparently had a special veneration.

THOMAS DE AQUINO. *Hystoria de corpore Christi. Vienna, Austria; 1403–1406; illuminated by Nikolaus of Brünn for Duke Wilhelm of Austria. 43 leaves (15 ¾ x 11¼ in.; 398 x 285 mm.). Frontispiece, 1 historiated initial. Gift of Mr. Louis M. Rabinowitz, 1951.*

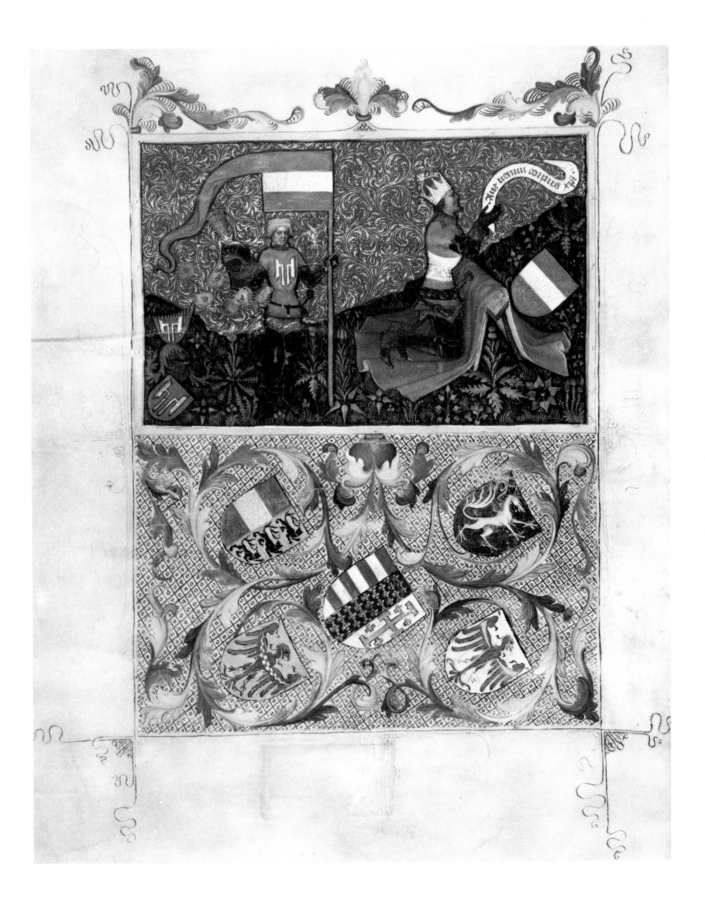

39

STAG HUNT

France, middle of the XV century [M.820, fol. 12]

The "Book of King Practice and Queen Theory," the first comprehensive hunting manual of the middle ages, was probably written by Henri de Ferrières (flourished 1350), whose name is hidden in a rebus at the end of a Modus manuscript in Paris (Bibliothèque Nationale, fr.12399). The Paris manuscript is dated 1379, is a copy of the original text, and is generally regarded as the finest Modus manuscript. A second rebus-bearing manuscript in the Bibliothèque Nationale (fr.1297), a copy of the first, is actually the textual prototype for the Morgan volume. The present codex is profusely illustrated: there are seventy-one miniatures which represent the work of at least two distinct artists. One of these exhibits a distant resemblance to the court style of René d'Anjou (for which see our number 37), and it is he who is responsible for the stag hunt shown here. The accompanying text advises the hunter to observe the directions of the turns taken by the stag during the chase, for the stag will be consistent in turning to the right or left. Such hunting scenes were also popularized by illustrated manuscripts of Gaston Phoebus' (1331–1391) *Le livre de la chasse*, which was written somewhat later than the Modus text. A richly illustrated example of about 1405–1410 is in Paris (Bibliothèque Nationale, fr.616).

HENRI DE FERRIÈRES. *Le livre du Roy Modus et de la Reine Ratio. Northern France; middle of the* xv *century. 160 leaves (11 5⁄8 x 8 3⁄4 in.; 295 x 223 mm.). 71 miniatures in tinted grisaille. Purchased in 1947.*

ase et ce te donna grant auisent
de toy retraire. Et prens garde
enchacant aquelle main le cerf
que tu chaceras se destournera
enfuyant ou adestre ou a sene
stix car il est de certam que en
faisant ses ruses il se destorne
voulentiers a vne main z celle
ou il se destourne m a m tent
tout se iour comunement.
¶ Ces deux choses que ie tay
dites donnent grant auisent
en chacant cest de sauoir les
ruses pendans et dauoir
auisement aquelle main ilz
se destournent. Car se tes
chiens chacent le contre ongle

cest adire se reuers par ou ilz
seront alez tu le sauras par les
ruses pendans et sidonment
auisement de retraire ses chies
pour deffaute la ruise. Puis
nous diuons coment len doit
relaissier au cerf ce que len
chace. ¶ Quant len enuoye
ses chiens au reles len y doit
enuoier tel qui ait congnois
sance du roy des sarges chiens
et la cause sy est que siloyent
venir aucune partie des chies
chacant combien que tous
ceulx que len auoit laisse
couuez ny feussent mie z qt
ny eust gaire de chiens et q

40

ANNUNCIATION

France, first decade of the XVI century [M.732, fol. 3v]

Le Grandes Heures d'Anne de Bretagne in Paris (Bibliothèque Nationale, lat.9474), the uncontested masterpiece of Jean Bourdichon of Tours, the last great French miniaturist, was probably finished about 1507–1508. Shortly thereafter at least three other manuscripts, all resembling the Bretagne Hours in style and decoration, were ordered. The first is in the British Museum (Add.Ms.18855), the second is now in the library at Waddesdon Manor (Ms.19), and the third is this fragmentary replica, which apparently had already left France by 1543, to judge by the added arms of Cristoforo Madruzzo (1512–1578), who was Prince Bishop and Cardinal of Trent in 1543. The fame and compositions of Bourdichon spread rapidly, and no less than four other Morgan Horae contain copies or variations of the Annunciation shown here. Delicately painted with care and accuracy, the miniatures create an ideal world seen through a Renaissance frame that is rarely captured in the workshop copies or derivations. The Annunciation illustrates Matins, the first Hour of the Virgin.

BOOK OF HOURS, *incomplete, use of Paris, in Latin. France, probably Tours; first decade of the* XVI *century; illuminated by Jean Bourdichon. 62 leaves (11⅞ x 7⅞ in.; 302 x 200 mm.). 8 full-page miniatures with fully bordered facing pages, 96 text pages with flowers and plants identified in Latin and French. Purchased in 1927.*

41

ADORATION OF THE MAGI

Spain, about 1470 [M.854, fol. 90v]

The achievements of early fifteenth-century Flemish painting, especially as embodied in the work of Jan van Eyck, had already had a great appeal to certain Spanish artists within Eyck's own lifetime. Louis Dalmau, for example, had gone to Ghent where he studied and copied Eyck's Ghent Altarpiece. This interest in the North continued in the second half of the century, where certain Castilian illuminators sought the most recent developments in their art. The illuminators of this manuscript, for example, had absorbed almost immediately the grisaille techniques that had been perfected by Flemish and French artists at that time. This influence can be seen in the borders shown here, where graduations of black, gray, gold, and white echo the subdued and somber color effects of the miniatures. The manuscript, according to heraldic and textual evidence, was made for the Infante Don Alfonso of Castile, the youngest brother of the future Queen Isabella, patroness of Columbus. Alfonso must have had a special veneration for St. John the Baptist, St. John the Evangelist, and Michael the Archangel, for these are accorded an unusual number of prayers and miniatures. Our reproduction shows the Adoration of the Magi, the standard illustration for Sext of the Hours of the Virgin.

BOOK OF HOURS, *use of Rome, in Latin. Spain, probably Toledo; about 1470; probably for the Infante Don Alfonso of Castile. 241 leaves (8¾ x 6⅜ in.; 224 x 162 mm.). 24 full-page and 8 smaller miniatures, 24 calendar illustrations, 1 portrait in border. Purchased with the assistance of the Fellows, 1951.*

42

VIRGO

Belgium, about 1403 [*M.785, fol. 16*]

This Virgo, represented as a lovely and courtly winged maiden holding a sheaf of grain, is but one of twelve full-page miniatures depicting the signs of the zodiac. While these illustrations are not heavily painted they are strongly drawn and delicately tinted. The text, an abridgement of Hermann the Dalmatian's mid-twelfth-century Latin translation from Albumasar's Arabic original, was compiled by the otherwise unknown Georgius Zothori Zapari Fenduli. Albumasar was a ninth-century astronomer-astrologer whom the middle ages honored as a prophet of Christ. Four other manuscripts, ranging over three centuries, are in the same family. The earliest is an Italian manuscript of the second quarter of the thirteenth century now in Paris (Bibliothèque Nationale, lat.7330). The immediate predecessor of the Morgan codex is a mid-fourteenth-century Franco-Flemish manuscript now in London (British Museum, Sloane Ms.3983). A successor, and close copy, is a mid-fifteenth-century French manuscript in Paris (Bibliothèque Nationale, lat.7331). The last, a still later French copy of about 1490, is now also in the Bibliothèque Nationale (Collection Smith-Lesouëf, Ms.8).

ALBUMASAR. *Astrological Treatises, in Latin. Bruges, Belgium; sometime before 7 June 1403, when Abbot Lubertus Hautschild, of St. Bartholomew's in Bruges, presented it to Jean, Duc de Berry. 52 leaves (10 x 6⅞ in.; 254 x 175 mm.). 76 full-page miniatures of zodiacal signs and the paranatellonta, and the planets in their houses, counter houses, exaltation, and in dejection. Purchased in 1935.*

Virgo   uir

43

THE APOSTLES ASSEMBLE AT THE VIRGIN'S HOUSE, THE APOSTLES BURY THE VIRGIN

Netherlands, about 1440 [M.868, fols. 59, 63]

This anonymous text is essentially a typological work which, like the *Biblia Pauperum*, connects Old and New Testament events. In this manuscript, however, no Old Testament scenes are shown, but excerpts from the Old Testament are written in the upper and lower margins of all the miniatures, except for the last six, which depict events related to the death of the Virgin. While depictions of the death of the Virgin were rather common in the fifteenth century, such extended narrative cycles, which detailed events slightly before and after her death, were rarer. The two shown here are among the most unusual: the miraculous assemblage of the apostles before the house of the Virgin, and the actual lowering of her coffin into the ground. Needless to say, these episodes, as well as the death of the Virgin itself, are not mentioned in the Bible, but depend on various apocryphal accounts which were popularized by such works as Jacobus de Voragine's Golden Legend, a compilation of the middle of the thirteenth century. The miniatures, which betray the influence of Italian art, especially in the use of green for the modelling of faces and flesh, are by an anonymous artist who may also have illustrated a Book of Hours in the Art Institute of Chicago (Ms.15.534).

SPIEGEL VAN DEN LEVEN ONS HEREN (*Mirror of the Life of Our Lord*), *and other religious texts, in Dutch. Netherlands, probably Brabant; about 1440. 89 leaves (7¾ x 5½ in.; 200 x 140 mm.). 42 full-page miniatures. Purchased in 1953.*

44

LAST JUDGMENT, KING DAVID

Netherlands, about 1410–1415 [*M.866, fols. 78v, 79*]

This Book of Hours belongs to a group of Horae all produced in the early years of the fifteenth century in the same north Netherlandish workshop. Other members of the group are in the University Library of Liège (Wittert Ms.35) and London (British Museum, Add.Ms.50005). A third, which was formerly in the collections of Sir Sydney Cockerell and Major J. R. Abbey, is currently in the possession of a New York dealer. Because of the mingling of various German, French, and Franco-Flemish elements in the products of this and other north Netherlandish schools, it has been fairly difficult to distinguish and localize them. Utrecht may have been the center for this school, however. The present manuscript contains a number of miniatures of unusual interest. The Bearing of the Cross, for example, includes the earliest depiction of the spikeblock, an instrument of torture attached either to Christ's robe or suspended from his waist to increase his suffering. In addition to the Hours of the Virgin and the Office of the Dead, Books of Hours frequently contain the Seven Penetential Psalms, which are here introduced by miniatures of the Last Judgment and King David. At the time this manuscript was made it was believed that David, who occupies the first letter of the first Penetential Psalm (*Domine* of Psalm VI), wrote them as penance for the Seven Capital Sins. Surrounding David are a series of interlocking monsters that anticipate the highly original borders found in the Hours of Catherine of Cleves, our next entry.

BOOK OF HOURS, *use of the Augustinian Canons of the Windesheim Chapter, in Latin. Netherlands, possibly Utrecht; about 1410–1415. 215 leaves (6¼ x 4¼ in.; 158 x 108 mm.). 53 full-page and 7 half-page miniatures, 24 calendar illustrations, 10 historiated initials, and numerous borders. Purchased with the assistance of the Fellows, 1953.*

45

DEVOTIONAL CRUCIFIXION, MOUTH OF HELL

Netherlands, about 1440 [M.917, p. 160; M.945, fol. 168v]

The best-known and one of the most important, not only of Dutch, but of all mediaeval manuscripts is the present Hours of Catherine of Cleves, which was made about 1440 for the Duchess of Guelders of the same name. Because it is one of the richest Books of Hours ever made, both from the point of view of its texts and cycles of illumination, many of which are not only unusual but unique, it is also a key monument in the history of Books of Hours. While the great artist who painted this manuscript remains anonymous—he is named the Master of Catherine of Cleves after this, his masterpiece—other works by his hand and workshop have been identified. The Hours of Aetzaert van Zaers in Leyden (Bibliotheek der Rijksuniversiteit, Ms.B.P.L.224) and part of a Dutch Bible of 1439 in Munich (Staatsbibliothek, Ms.germ.1102) are by his hand, while a prayerbook in the Hague (Rijksmuseum Meermanno-Westreenianum, Ms.10.E.1), though closely related, may be a workshop production. The history of the manuscript—how it was broken up into two parts and sold as separate and complete Horae, and how, after one part had been offered to the Morgan Library and purchased in 1963, it was recognized by John Plummer that it was actually part of another seemingly complete Horae then in the Guennol Collection—is all admirably recounted in the color facsimile of all the miniatures that was published in 1966. In 1970 both parts of the Cleves Hours were finally reunited under the same roof, though they had already been brought together earlier in Plummer's facsimile, where the original sequence of the miniatures had been painstakingly reconstructed. Shown here are two miniatures, one from each part. The first is an unusual devotional Crucifixion containing a hierarchy of intercessions on behalf of Catherine of Cleves, all of which are explained by inscriptions. Catherine of Cleves, introduced by an unidentified patron saint, implores the Mother of God to pray for her. The Virgin, with her breast exposed as a reminder to Christ that she nursed Him, intercedes on Catherine's behalf. Christ, in turn, in the name of His wounds, asks His Father to spare Catherine. He responds that His Son's prayer has been heard with favor. The miniature illustrates the Saturday Mass of the Virgin. Our second illustration comes from the Office of the Dead, which is generally introduced by some aspect of the funeral ceremony, but which here depicts a highly imaginative and surprising Mouth of Hell. The façade of the gate of hell, populated by demons who torture and mutilate souls, actually consists of three mouths flanked by towers which are surmounted by cauldrons. In the border below, scrolls listing the Seven Deadly Sins issue from the mouth of a green demon.

[CONTINUED]

BOOK OF HOURS, *use of the Augustinian Canons of the Windesheim Chapter, in Latin. Utrecht, Netherlands; about 1440; illuminated by the Master of Catherine of Cleves for Catherine of Cleves, Duchess of Guelders.* M.917: *328 pages (7⁹⁄₁₆ x 5 ⅛ in.; 192 x 130 mm.); 10 full-page and 84 smaller miniatures, with many unusual borders. Purchased on the Belle da Costa Greene Fund and with the assistance of the Fellows, 1963.* M.945: *193 leaves (7⁹⁄₁₆ x 5 ⅛ in.; 192 x 130 mm.); 15 full-page and 48 smaller miniatures, with many scenes in the borders. Purchased on the Belle da Costa Greene Fund, and with the assistance of the Fellows, and special assistance of Mrs. Frederick B. Adams, Sr., Mrs. Robert Charles, Mr. Laurens M. Hamilton, The Heineman Foundation, Mrs. Donald F. Hyde, Mrs. Jacob M. Kaplan, Mrs. John Kean, Mr. Paul Mellon, Mr. and Mrs. Charles F. Morgan, Mr. Lessing J. Rosenwald, Mr. and Mrs August H. Schilling, Mrs. Herbert N. Straus, Mrs. Landon K. Thorne, Mrs. Alan Valentine, and Mr. and Mrs. Arnold Whitridge, and Miss Julia B. Wightman, 1970.*

46

SCRIBES AND PHARISEES CONSPIRE AGAINST CHRIST

Belgium, about 1485 [M.894, fol. 108v]

The Scribes and Pharisees Conspire against Christ and a large portion of the other miniatures in this Life of Christ may well represent the finest work of an artist who has now
come to be known as the Master of Edward IV. This master, whose miniatures have all
the complexity, detail, and vigour of panel paintings, was active in Bruges in the 1470s
and 1480s, and seems to have specialized in the illumination of exceptionally large manuscripts written in the vernacular. The present manuscript, a *Cyropédie* of Xenophon in
Brussels (Bibliothèque Royale, Ms.11703), and a *Histoire d'Alexandre* of Quintus Curtius
in Geneva (Bibliothèque Publique et Universitaire, Ms.76) were all made for members
of the Oettingen family. The artist takes his name from a *Bible historiale* in London
(British Museum, Mss. Royal 18 D IX, X) which he illustrated for King Edward IV in
1479.

LUDOLPHUS DE SAXONIA, *Vita Christi, Part 3 only of the French translation by Guillaume le Menant.
Bruges, Belgium; about 1485; illuminated by the Master of Edward IV for Johann, Count of Oettingen. 249
leaves (18½ x 13 in.; 470 x 331 mm.). 50 large miniatures, 1 elaborate border. Gift of Mrs. Edgar S. Oppen-
heimer in memory of her husband, 1960.*

47

VISITATION, RESURRECTION

Italy, about 1420 [*M.944, fols. 52v, 26v*]

These two miniatures and twenty others, all of which illustrate the liturgically arranged prayers in this manuscript, form the largest body of paintings by Michelino Molinari da Besozzo that survive. Before the discovery of this manuscript, his masterpiece, his work was known only through two small panels, some drawings, and several miniatures in manuscripts. These include a signed panel of the Mystic Marriage of St. Catherine in Siena (National Gallery) and manuscripts in London (British Museum, Egerton Ms.3266), Paris (Bibliothèque Nationale, lat.5888), and Avignon (Bibliothèque Municipale, Ms. 111). Documents in the Cathedral of Milan also mention him as a master of stained glass and a painter of frescoes, but none of these works survive. From such superbly preserved miniatures as the Visitation (celebrated on 2 July) and the Resurrection (Easter Sunday) one can now better judge the contemporary references to this versatile Michelino as the "supreme painter" and "the most excellent of all the painters in the world."

PRAYERBOOK, *in Latin. Milan, Italy; about 1420; illuminated by Michelino da Besozzo. 95 leaves (6¾ x 4¾ in.; 170 x 120 mm.). 22 full-page miniatures with floral borders, 47 text pages with floral borders by a second hand. 1 historiated initial, 46 illuminated initials. Purchased with the generous assistance of Miss Alice Tully in memory of Dr. Edward Graeffe, 1970.*

Resurrecao ihu xpi. gloria.

Salutacio virginis et elisabeth.

48

ST. LAWRENCE

Germany, 1507 [M.905, I, fol. 88]

Illuminated liturgical books generally exhibit a hierarchy of decoration; the most important texts or feasts are introduced by the largest and finest miniatures. If there are no large miniatures, such as in this manuscript, the hierarchy begins at a lower level; the most important feasts have historiated initials and elaborate borders, while the lesser feasts have nonfigural decoration or none at all. It is thus not surprising that the only saint to receive a historiated initial here (within the C of *Confessio*) is St. Lawrence, the patron of the church in Nuremberg for which the manuscript was made. The codex, known as the "Geese Book" because it contains a border scene where a fox conducts a choir of geese, is actually a Gradual, a choir book containing the music for the Mass. Although the two signed and dated volumes of the Gradual do not represent Jacob Elsner's most important work, they are significant because they document his development from 1507 to 1510, the years preceding his most important commission, a Missal of 1513, which is still owned by the descendants of the man who ordered it and the "Geese Book," Anton Kress.

GRADUAL, *in Latin. Nuremberg, Germany; 1507 and 1510; written by Friedrich Rosendorn and illuminated by Jacob Elsner for the provost of St. Lorenz, Anton Kress. Vol. I: 261 leaves (25 ¾ x 17¼ in.; 654 x 438 mm.). 7 large historiated initials, 11 illuminated initials, 18 decorated borders, some with scenes. Vol. II: 299 leaves (25 ¾ x 17½ in.; 654 x 445 mm.). 11 large historiated initials, 8 illuminated initials, 19 decorated borders, some with scenes. Gift of the Samuel H. Kress Foundation, 1962.*

49

CRUCIFIXION

Germany, about 1510 [M.955, fol. 1v]

Before the discovery of this Crucifixion, all that had been known of the first volume of the Missal of Bishop Hugo von Hohenlandenberg, from which this leaf comes, were eleven historiated initials. They had been attributed to Hans Springinklee, a pupil of Albrecht Dürer. While this attribution has been questioned, there is little doubt that this leaf, the artistic masterpiece of the volume, was by an artist who was influenced by Dürer. His paintings and watercolors are recalled by the transparent and luminous quality of the colors found in the drapery and landscape. The striking similarity of the drapery and stance of St. John with that of a St. John panel in Cologne (Wallraf-Richartz-Museum) ascribed to Georg Pencz, also a Dürer student, provides yet another connection with his workshop. Since the panel is dated about 1525–1527, however, either a dependency or common prototype is implied.

MISSAL LEAF. *Constance, Germany; about 1510; apparently the Canon illustration from the first of a four-volume Missal commissioned by Bishop Hugo von Hohenlandenberg of Constance, whose arms occur on this leaf. (The first volume was sold in 1832 and later broken up; 11 leaves with historiated initials are now on loan to the Rosgarten Museum in Constance. The remaining volumes, all intact, are now in the Archiepiscopal Diocesan Archive in Freiburg i.Br.) 1 leaf (16 x 11⅜ in.; 407 x 289 mm.). Purchased as the gift of the Fellows, with the special assistance of four members of the Board of Trustees, Mrs. Gordon S. Rentschler, and the Arkville Erpf Fund, 1973, in honor of the Fiftieth Anniversary of the Library.*

LONG-HAIRED BUT SHORT-WITTED MAIDENS

Austria, last quarter of the XV century [M.763, fol. 8v]

Hugo von Trimberg, who was an instructor for forty years at Teurstadt, near Bamberg, probably excerpted materials for his lengthy *Der Renner* from his own collection of Latin and German manuscripts. The allegorical and moralizing tales that make up *Der Renner* were taken from such sources as the Bible, Aesop's and other fables, bestiaries, and the classical authors. Although the work was completed by 1200, additions continued to be made until 1313. The illustration reproduced here is taken from his chapter on maidens, where he speaks of their long hair, short wit, and changeability of mood—one day they may be attracted to dark young men, the next, to blond ones. The two maidens, one in formal, the other in normal dress, hold a scroll which in the Leyden manuscript (Bibliotheek der Rijksuniversiteit, Ms.Voss.germ.-gal. fol. 4) of about 1401–1402 contains a German inscription which says, "Our thoughts change often." The two maidens are remarkably close to St. Anne and her attendant in a Birth of the Virgin panel in Innsbruck (Ferdinandeum), which has been attributed to the Tyrolian Master of the Uttenheim Panels.

HUGO VON TRIMBERG. *Der Renner, in German. Austria, probably in the Tyrol; last quarter of the* xv *century. 263 leaves of paper (11 ½ x 8 ⅛ in.; 293 x 207 mm.). 30 full-page and 61 half-page miniatures. Purchased in 1930.*

pej den ich selluch icht guets vinde
Deit smähen trautz hohuart ist
so lat euch sagen in kurtz fast
von manig vnwirdigs smähen
vor horn vnd auch sehen
Von manig stolltzhait
der hertz enpor die hohuart trait
Vnd lat euch bescharden
Zu dem ersten von den maiden

BIBLIOGRAPHICAL NOTE

For information on manuscripts acquired in the last fifty years the following works may be consulted:

1. Seymour de Ricci, *Census of Medieval and Renaissance Manuscripts in the United States and Canada*, New York, 1935–1937 (to M.793).

C. U. Faye and W. H. Bond, *Supplement*, New York, 1962 (M.794–M.881; with additional bibliography for earlier numbers).

2. *The Pierpont Morgan Library. A Review of Acquisitions 1949–1968*, New York, 1969 (M.831–M.939).

3. More extensive discussions of principal acquisitions may be found in these four *Reviews*:

The Pierpont Morgan Library. A Review of the Growth, Development and Activities of the Library during the Period between its Establishment as an Educational Institution in February 1924 and the Close of the Year 1929, New York, 1930.

The Pierpont Morgan Library. Review of the Activities and Acquisitions of the Library from 1930 through 1935, New York, 1937.

The Pierpont Morgan Library. Review of the Activities and Acquisitions of the Library from 1936 through 1940, New York, 1941.

The Pierpont Morgan Library. Review of the Activities and Major Acquisitions of the Library 1941–1948, New York, 1949.

4. Since the founding of the Fellows of the Pierpont Morgan Library in 1949, sixteen *Reports* have been published between the years 1950 and 1973. Whereas the first fifteen of these only included discussions of the principal acquisitions, the *Sixteenth Report to the Fellows of the Pierpont Morgan Library 1969–1971*, New York, 1973, the first issued under the present Director, now includes a Check List which contains descriptions of all the manuscripts acquired during the years covered by the *Report*. This Check List, in addition to describing the textual and pictorial contents of each manuscript, also provides an up-to-date bibliography. These Check Lists will be included in all future *Reports*, which, for the first time, will be available to the public.

5. Three large and important exhibition catalogues are also useful:

The Pierpont Morgan Library, Exhibition of Illuminated Manuscripts Held at the New York Public Library, New York, 1934.

Italian Manuscripts in the Pierpont Morgan Library, compiled by Meta Harrsen and George K. Boyce, New York, 1953. Of the 103 illuminated manuscripts, twenty-four were acquired after 1924. Nineteen more have been acquired since the publication of the catalogue.

Central European Manuscripts in the Pierpont Morgan Library, compiled by Meta Harrsen, New York, 1958. Of the sixty-four illuminated manuscripts twenty-eight were acquired after 1924. Ten more have been acquired since the publication of the catalogue.

6. Three important collections of manuscripts and papyri are on deposit at the Library, and these have all been catalogued:

The Colt Greek and Arabic Papyri: L. Casson, E. L. Hettich, and C. J. Kraemer, Jr., *Excavations at Nessana*, II–III, Princeton, 1950–1958.

Five illuminated manuscripts were deposited with the collection of Dannie N. Heineman: *Books and Manuscripts from the Heineman Collection*, New York, 1963.

The William S. Glazier Collection, containing seventy-five manusctips: *The Glazier Collection of Illuminated Manuscripts*, compiled by John Plummer, New York, 1968.

CONCORDANCE OF MANUSCRIPTS

The first number is the Morgan number, and the second is the catalogue number. The plate numbers are identical with the catalogue numbers.

692 – 15	730 – 19	776 – 1	820 – 39	868 – 43
700 – 25	732 – 40	777 – 12	827 – 7	869 – 6
705 – 37	736 – 13	780 – 11	828 – 27	883 – 14
708 – 9	739 – 24	781 – 10	834 – 36	893 – 34
709 – 8	740 – 26	785 – 42	853 – 38	894 – 46
710 – 20	754 – 29	791 – 16	854 – 41	905 – 48
711 – 21	755 – 5	800 – 32	855 – 23	917 – 45
713 – 33	756 – 17	805 – 28	860 – 4	944 – 47
722 – 30	763 – 50	806 – 28	862 – 2	945 – 45
728 – 3	769 – 31	807 – 28	866 – 44	955 – 49
729 – 18	775 – 35	808 – 22		

PRODUCED BY

THE STINEHOUR PRESS

AND

THE MERIDEN GRAVURE COMPANY